Steve Parish
PUBLISHING

A Wild Australia Guide

WILDLIFE
PHOTOGRAPHY

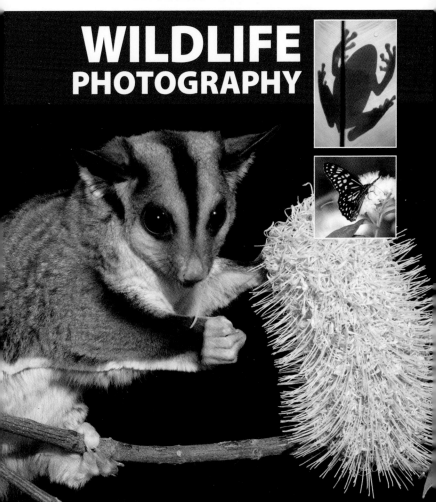

STEVE PARISH

Contents

Left: All creatures, regardless of how common they might be, provide endless challenges to a serious nature photographer. Here, an Australian Magpie lets all within earshot know that he is the "boss" of his territory *(35 mm SLR, 80–400 mm zoom lens, 1/250 f 5.6, Velvia ISO 100, flash fill).*

Introduction

Photographing Australian wildlife can be a very addictive pastime — one that can provide a dedicated photographer with a life-long interest. There are countless species, each with its own story to tell, meaning the challenge is endless. Because there are so many species, there are just as many things to learn about how to approach and photograph each one. But what would life be like without an interesting challenge?

Regardless of whether your camera is an SLR or a compact camera, or what lenses you have, the three factors that are most important when photographing wildlife are content, mood and design (CMD). The content of a photograph refers to the subject and what makes it unique. Are there elements that, if included in a composition, will make a picture even more powerful? Mood is a combination of lighting and the effects you have used to create an image, such as selective focus and flash fill-in. Design is multifaceted, involving composition, angle of view and colour. Every time you approach a subject, try to consider CMD — as time passes you will find that you will be concentrating on these factors subconsciously.

I have focused this guide on field technique, with only a small section on the digital post-production world, because there are numerous books that deal with that subject. This book is designed to introduce you to each aspect of wildlife photography and show you how to vary your photographs from the perspective of equipment and field technique. You will find that many aspects of wildlife photography are similar for different species, so moving from one group of animals to another does not necessarily mean you need to invest in different equipment.

I hope this *Wild Australia Guide* inspires you to become involved in this satisfying pastime — a pastime that with today's instant digital results, will enable you to share your discoveries with those around you. We owe it to Australia's wonderful wildlife to promote and appreciate their existence in our world and to care for the habitats in which they live.

Note: Apart from a few underwater pictures, all of the photographs in this book were taken with 35 mm cameras. Some were exposed with film and others were taken digitally and are shown as either SLR or DSLR. I have also recorded the shutter speeds and the f-stop numbers (or aperture), the lens used, the ISO of the film or digital setting and the type of digital file. The majority of the photographs have been taken in the wild — those animals that were photographed in captivity have been identified as such.

Opposite, top: The delicate flutter of a Cairns Birdwing Butterfly. **Above, clockwise from top left:** An intricately patterned Emperor Angelfish; A Sugar Glider sips at sweet grevillea nectar; Ambling Echidna; The curious and colourful Crimson Rosella; A Frilled Lizard hissing; The Orange-eyed Tree-frog; Dainty feather stars attached to a gorgonian sea fan *(all photographs taken with a 35 mm SLR camera)*.

Cameras for Wildlife Photography

In writing my photography books, it is not my intention to influence your choice of brand or model in any way. Most brands target one or more markets — each loosely defined as certain types of "buyer". Models are designed (in terms of the features they possess) according to research into the "target market's" needs. Camera models are then priced accordingly — the more sophisticated the features, the higher the price. Features include motor drives, setting options, pixel size or zoom magnification, for instance.

The price people will pay for a camera is influenced by the results they hope to achieve. Are you wanting to enjoy photography as a pastime? Or do you hope to become a professional photographer? There is a lot of choice in the marketplace, but ultimately your decision should be based on your needs and your budget. Generally, in order to be competitive, the top brands offer similar features and try to keep their pricing within a realistic range. Of course, once you start using a particular brand and invest in that brand's lenses, and you're happy with your photos, you will most likely stick with that brand (this is why I have stuck with the same brand for 30 years for my wildlife photographic work).

It is natural to assume that the more you pay for a camera, the better the pictures will be. This is not the case. *People* take pictures, cameras do not. Higher-priced cameras may have extra features that offer a wide range of alternatives — however, a simple approach to wildlife photography may be just as effective. I would advise amateurs to assess their needs and stick to a set budget. Some experienced film photographers who are new to digital photography believe they should wait until they can afford the "top of the range" digital SLR (DSLR). Another mistake, in my opinion. Many lower-priced compact cameras have excellent lenses and sensor quality that matches the higher-priced digital SLRs. In fact, one of my associates uses compact cameras exclusively because of their size, weight and ease of operation. He is a naturalist and finds this camera ideal for photographing everything from landscapes to macro close-ups. In fact, his pictures are unique and of such high quality that I publish many in our specialist wildlife books. His is a fine example of "knowing your animal", which is often more important than having a top of the range camera. I must say, however, that he is restricted in how much he can manage the outcome of his pictures.

Another advantage of many compact digital cameras is their live LCD screen, which allows you to view your composition, focus and colour as you take the photograph. This is excellent for photographing frogs, reptiles and insects or any animal on the ground. In some cases, LCD screens can be rotated, enabling you to take images in awkward places or close to the ground. Nonetheless, there is no argument that digital SLR cameras offer the greatest range of features. The quality of some inexpensive models has also placed these cameras within the reach of most amateurs.

Above: When I am wandering around during the day, I usually carry two cameras. One has a 80–400 mm zoom lens, the other a wide-angle zoom that also enables close-ups. This is an ideal way to "kit up" when you just don't know what you will encounter. On this three hour stroll at Glen Helen Gorge in central Australia there were great landscapes, and small bush birds, like the Zebra Finch (top right). If you get there early before human voices filter through the gorge, you may even find an Australian Grebe (centre right), ducks or egrets among the sedges. There is also an abundance of insects attracted by the water. If you do not have a second camera, or additional lenses with you, it can be very frustrating when shots are missed.

Telephoto lenses make a distant subject look larger — in other words, distance is compressed. Anything longer than 70 mm is considered to be telephoto. The shorter telephoto lenses (between 70 mm and 200 mm) are ideal for photographing larger animals such as kangaroos or waterbirds in parks. Lenses from 300 mm to around 600 mm on 135 formats are ideal for wildlife.

The shorter 300 mm and 400 mm lenses are small enough to be handheld, with shutter speeds in excess of 1/250th of a second. If the lens has an image stabiliser system built in, then hand holding may be adequate down to as slow as 1/100th of a second. The 500 mm or 600 mm lenses on both small and medium-format cameras require either a monopod or tripod.

The telephoto lens is certainly my favourite lens and I use one for everything from landscapes to flower close-ups. The optics of a long telephoto lens create a wonderful sense of compression and, by shooting with the lens at its maximum aperture, it is possible to create soft backgrounds. Using a telephoto lens, foregrounds that might normally spoil an image can be softened to enhance the picture.

When you are weighing up what size focal length lens you need, be sure to assess the wide range of zoom lenses that are available. Lenses with zoom ranges of 70–300 mm are available in quality brands. However, if you are specialising in long lens work for publishing, particularly when lenses beyond 300 mm are to be used, then fixed focal length lenses are preferable.

If you find your budget is being stretched, you might consider a tele-converter. The better converters, used with higher quality lenses, will produce good results. They are available for most telephoto lenses. Two are available for the camera I use. One effectively increases the focal length by 100% but reduces speed by two f-stops; the other increases the focal length by 40% and only one f-stop is lost. The latter is ideal, because by pushing my ISO one f-stop and converting my 500 mm lens to 700 mm, I obtain almost identical results to the longer lens. I find, 700 mm is a perfect focal length for photographing most shy birds and animals.

Close-up Lenses

I have used close-up lens attachments, macro tubes and macro lenses over the years, and can say with some certainty that I would never run out of subjects. If I shot close-up every day for the rest of my life, magnifying small insects, frogs, reptiles and flowers, I would never tire of the subject matter. If you want adventure, there are entire worlds in the undergrowth or beneath the sea that offer a lifetime of challenges for a close-up photographer.

There are a number of ways to "tool up" for macro work and, depending on your price range, each has a specific benefit. Naturally enough, the largest array of close-up attachments, lenses and extension rings applies only to SLR interchangeable lens systems. Compact cameras, which are restricted to range-finder viewing, do not have threads for the attachment of close-up equipment, especially on zoom lenses, but it is possible to use close-up filters attached to the camera body or to a tripod. Most digital camera brands now feature an LCD viewing system — a facility that assists with close-up photography. Although many modern lenses have the ability to focus close-up, they will never achieve the level of magnification, or the optical quality, of a macro lens that has been specifically designed for the purpose of macro photography.

Right and below: The outcome of insect photography obtained with the use of a close-up lens. With patience and a good eye, intricate detail can be achieved.

Above: With a 750 mm lens and an electronic flash, I have been able to fill in the harsh, dark shadows from a distance of ten metres — all done automatically!

The principal reason for using electronic flash is to provide light where very poor or no light exists; hence the nickname "electronic sunshine". However, light is not the only advantage of flash photography — the modern flash, known as a strobe by underwater photographers, offers many advantages for a creative photographer.

Gone are the days of estimating exposure with electronic flashes — now the camera and the electronic flash do all the calculating for you with the aid of sophisticated, computerised electronics in the flash unit and the camera. There are four primary kinds of flash — those that are built into and powered by the camera's power source; the detachable flash, usually mounted onto the camera's hot shoe, which houses its own power source; the separate, portable flash unit (often used by professional photographers in studios) which usually has a separate power source; and finally, the macro flash which is mounted on the front of the lens.

Each flash has the facility for attaching reflectors or diffusers which assist photographers when they use "modelling light" to preview the flashlighting, or when adjusting the power to reduce the light's intensity. When fill-in flash is used creatively along with daylight (whatever the conditions) for modelling or illuminating/softening shadows, there will be no evidence at all of artificial light. If you do not have diffusers or reflectors, you can always use white or coloured cardboard. I often use flash fill-in for wildflower and insect photography and the effect can be so subtle that I have many shots which are indistinguishable from those in which only natural light was used. Apart from the obvious uses (underwater and at night), it is the photographer's prerogative to use artificial lighting as a creative tool, much like any other accessory.

POSITIONING THE FLASH

The position of your electronic flash depends on how the subject is illuminated. When you are photographing mammals, such as these Common Ringtail Possums (right), red-eye (an effect caused by having your electronic flash attached to the camera and directly in alignment with the lens) can be a problem. It can be avoided by detaching the flash unit and moving it slightly away from the lens's angle of view.

MULTIPLE FLASH TECHNIQUE

To make the photo of a Giant Cave Gecko (left), I held one flash with my left hand. An assistant held a second flash behind the animal, at an angle of around 45° to my camera, so that the light did not pass directly into my lens. It is possible to wirelessly connect flash units, each managed by a central control unit.

FILL-IN FLASH

Balanced fill-in flash is achieved when the power of the flash is set to correspond with the available natural light, so that neither overrides the other. The effect, seen in this photo of Superb Fairy-wrens (right), adds detail by filling in harsh shadows, reducing contrast between light and shade (particularly when shooting towards the sun) and enhancing colour.

MACRO FLASH

My through-the-lens (TTL) metering macro electronic flash system delivered the illumination in this ultra close-up shot of an Orange-eyed Tree-frog (left). Like most frogs, they have a habit of hopping just when you have the flashes all set-up and angled in the right direction. In these circumstances, the macro flash system is ideal.

Different weather conditions create a variety of lighting conditions, which suit different kinds of photographic subjects. Overcast weather, which does not throw dense shadows, is ideal for photographing in woodlands, shrublands and rainforests. On bright, sunny days, an experienced photographer would most likely change their plans, preferring to shoot on the coast or in more open surrounds.

DIFFUSED LIGHT

If cloud cover, mist, dust or some other sort of haze is diffusing the light, do not despair — this type of light is perfect for a range of photographic subjects. Fine particles in the air soften the landscape, which can enhance the mood in an image. I find misty and hazy days beneficial for close-up or telephoto work with wildflowers and wildlife, or when shooting inside a forest. In these instances, harsh sunlight creates dark shadows that can make a photograph unappealing; whereas filtered light reflecting from fine particles in the air can gently illuminate even the darkest corners.

Overcast weather can also bring with it cooler conditions, which can cause wildlife to become more active. Nocturnal mammals may remain out longer in the early morning, or may emerge earlier in the evening due to the lowered light level. Some birds are also more active during the middle of a sunless day. In addition, the silver lining to cloudy weather is that it softens light, making the minute details of intricate fur and feathers far more defined.

Another effect of diffused light is intensified colour. This can be seen when bright areas of sky are excluded from the frame. As a result of the lack of shadow and contrast, colours appear more tonally varied and fine textures are visible. The subject's form is more likely to be enhanced in diffused light, especially if the photographic angle is varied. To select the best angle, simply try moving around your subject.

HARSH MIDDAY LIGHT

The main problem associated with working while the sun is high; is contrast in light and shade which can produce deep, dark, unattractive shadows and colours that have little tonal variation. However, I have found I can extend my working time and shoot throughout the day by carefully choosing my subject, lens and angle of view. Another advantage can be that you are able to use fast shutter speeds and small aperture openings, which enables you to freeze action and retain depth of field, as seen in the photograph of the active Little Egrets (above).

THE GLOW OF SUNRISE & SUNSET

In the rich glow that accompanies most sunrises and sunsets, colours are usually warmer and wild creatures are more likely to be out and about. The beginning and end of the day are my favourite times to photograph (I don't think one is any better than the other) and I often wish these fleeting, gleaming times would last forever.

Haze, which is common at these times of day, coupled with the angle of the rising or setting sun, can produce some spectacular images. Photographs of any wildlife subject, whether distant or close-up, will be rendered stunning in light that has such special, evocative qualities. At dawn, the sun's rays may have to penetrate mist or fog, producing wonderfully soft, moody images — particularly when the sun is included in the composition. At sunset, the day's dust reflects the dying light and softens the world's hard edges.

Waterbirds and sea birds, photographed on wet sand or across the mirrored surface of a billabong, cast reflections that can add to the drama of a picture. Depending on your angle of view to the sun, you may also be able to use silhouettes (such as in the photo below), coupled with twilight colour, to create magnificent photographs.

Equipment & Accessories

Your photographic goals will determine just what accessories you need, but two pieces of equipment are essential for wildlife photography — the tripod and the monopod. Like cameras, they come in an array of choices, particularly tripods.

Tripods   Depending on the work you intend to do, you may need several tripods and each should be selected on its weight, flexibility (particularly adjustable height) and head movement. Do not be tempted by cheap models. A quality tripod is a tool that you will probably find yourself using all day long. Beware tripods that have heads and legs with fidgety adjustments, as these can be very frustrating. I prefer a smaller, lightweight tripod for bush walks.

Monopods   These are relatively simple and straightforward and are used mainly for shooting with long lenses when light is reasonably bright, allowing faster shutter speeds to be used.

Cable Releases   When you are assessing tripods for purchase, be sure to consider cable releases, which come in varying lengths. A cable release is essential for shutter releases of 1/15th of a second and slower. A long cable is handy as the shutter can be released and tripod positioned with one hand, whilst focusing with the other. If your camera has a built-in time delay, a cable release may not be needed.

Above, clockwise from top: Ball/socket head with snap-on camera attachment; A lightweight tripod; A lightweight monopod.

TRIPOD & MONOPOD CONSIDERATIONS

The large, professional tripod head shown left is an excellent example of what I would recommend for most photographic situations. This unit has a snap-on coupling, so, provided your cameras have the corresponding connection, they can be quickly attached.

Select a professional, lightweight, carbon tripod that extends to 2 m. Extension is very important because when you are angling a long lens upwards at about 45°, you need to be able to look through the viewfinder without bending your back. You may have to stand for hours waiting for a bird to return and you do not want to be bending over every time you need to look through the lens. Also note that the legs on your tripod or monopod can be independently adjusted, which is important because you will rarely be working on level terrain.

There are many brands and models available. The ones pictured are from Velbon.

CAMERA CASES

I must admit, I am a bit of a sucker for camera cases. I have a room full of them! There are sizes and shapes to suit every piece of equipment or configuration imaginable.

When I am working, I frequently carry entire systems (DSLRs and video) in large Pelican™ cases in the back of my vehicle. If I am flying interstate and hiring a vehicle, then these robust cases are perfect.

On the back seat of the car I have soft, smaller backpacks kitted up for each set of gear. If I am leaving the car to walk, I think about what I am likely to encounter and set-up a suitable bag. I also pack a range of "just in case" equipment. If I am travelling long distances, I re-pack the gear into the aforementioned heavy-duty cases and secure them to the car floor. Secure packing is essential for your equipment to ensure it will not be damaged. For example, I once packed a 600 mm lens wrapped in towels and packed in a soft bag, by air from Gladstone to Brisbane. When it arrived, I found the lens broken clean off the camera body!

PACK & CARRY SYSTEMS

I find the hard-shelled and padded interior of the Pelican™ case, and the soft, padded and zippered Lowepro™ bags ideal for my needs. However, there are bags and cases of every size and shape to suit every occasion. The Omni Trekker Extreme™ range is worth considering because these bags are designed to fit inside the Pelican™ cases, a perfect solution for air travel or transportation to and from boats at sea. The Pelican™ case provides the robust waterproof protection needed and your "treasures" nestle safely inside the bag. When you arrive on location, you only have to pull out the inner case and it converts into a backpack. These are, of course, only suggestions and it is best to do your own research to find the best solution for your requirements.

Climate & Wildlife

Australia is so large and its climate so varied that it can be difficult to choose the time frame for your journey. Particularly, if you intend to travel a long way, across distinctly separate regions, over a short period. There is no single "ideal season" to travel in both northern and southern Australia. To complicate matters further, seasonal conditions vary widely between coastal and inland regions, mountains and plains and from year to year. The key is to study each region's climate carefully, and leave detailed scheduling until as late as possible prior to departure. Even

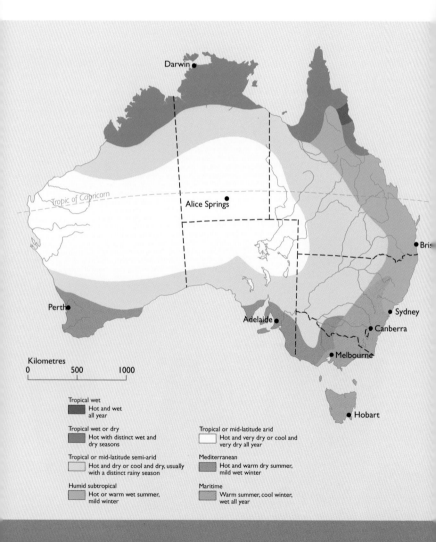

Kilometres
0   500   1000

Tropical wet
Hot and wet
all year

Tropical wet or dry
Hot with distinct wet and
dry seasons

Tropical or mid-latitude semi-arid
Hot and dry or cool and dry, usually
with a distinct rainy season

Humid subtropical
Hot or warm wet summer,
mild winter

Tropical or mid-latitude arid
Hot and very dry or cool and
very dry all year

Mediterranean
Hot and warm dry summer,
mild wet winter

Maritime
Warm summer, cool winter,
wet all year

then, you should be prepared to change your plans as the weather dictates. In the wet season of Australia's Tropical North, dried up creekbeds can turn to swollen, flooding rivers almost overnight and insufficient planning can result in huge delays or worse. To assist you in mapping out your journey, the information listed below gives you some general guidelines to the climatic conditions you are likely to encounter in various regions throughout the year.

TROPICAL WET, WET OR DRY & HUMID SUBTROPICAL REGIONS

December to late February can be very wet across Australia's north and roads can often become impassable. Due to the abundance of water, wildlife disperses over large areas. Temperatures and humidity will be high and it can rain for days on end. In coastal, savanna and hinterland regions, tropical cyclones can unleash destructive winds and torrential rain.

March, April and May can be very pretty. Grasses are still green, waterholes are full and lilies are in bloom. Waterbirds and bush birds congregate around the gradually shrinking watercourses. There is less rain in these months, but the weather remains humid. This can also be a good time for invertebrates.

June through to late August is the coolest period and, for this reason, these months become the peak tourist season.

September to December is the dry season and is an excellent time for finding wildlife around waterholes and in national parks, but it can be hot, smoky and dusty.

TROPICAL OR MID-LATITUDE ARID & SEMI-ARID REGIONS

October to March are the hot months in arid areas — so hot that travel and camping can be most unpleasant. The wildflowers will have died off and the flora lost its green lustre.

April and May are the earliest months to think of travelling in the dry, hot centre of Australia; however, June through to September can be the time when flowering and wildlife are the most prolific. This will depend on how much rain has fallen in previous months.

"MEDITERRANEAN" REGIONS

The "Mediterranean" regions of Australia have hot, dry summers and mild, wet winters. Vast coastal heathlands are usually covered with abundant wildflowers from late August and during the spring months of September, October and November in these regions.

May, June and July are the cooler, wetter months and the wind can blow endlessly at this time. Late spring (October and November) and late summer (February, extending to autumnal March) are wonderful times for wildlife, although I always tend to focus on the spring months when flowering in the woodlands and heathlands attracts many birds and insects. This time of the year is also when many mammals breed.

MARITIME REGIONS

This climatic type includes some of the nation's most picturesque regions, such as the Blue Mountains, the Australian Alps and the far south-eastern coast. My preferred season for photographing wildlife is spring, but if snowy or alpine scenes are to your liking, then the winter months of June, July and August are best. The summer months (December–February) can be very hot, with heat haze and bushfire smoke common, even in cities. The weather in Tasmania, one of the nation's best States for temperate wildlife photography, can vary enormously. Not a cloud in the sky at dawn, by midday raining, and hot by late afternoon.

Habitat & Wildlife

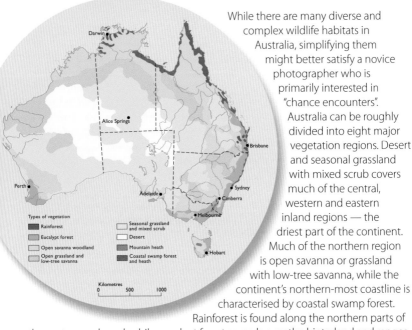

While there are many diverse and complex wildlife habitats in Australia, simplifying them might better satisfy a novice photographer who is primarily interested in "chance encounters". Australia can be roughly divided into eight major vegetation regions. Desert and seasonal grassland with mixed scrub covers much of the central, western and eastern inland regions — the driest part of the continent. Much of the northern region is open savanna or grassland with low-tree savanna, while the continent's northern-most coastline is characterised by coastal swamp forest. Rainforest is found along the northern parts of the eastern seaboard, while eucalypt forest spreads over the hinterland and ranges of the east, south-east and south-west coasts. Tasmania features a mix of vegetation, including mountain heath.

These primary habitats dictate the species of animal you are likely to find. There are, of course, many bird and insect species that occupy what is known as "micro-habitat". These species often feed primarily on only one plant or just a few species of plant, which may be both seasonal and habitat-specific.

📷 QUICK TIP

- A great way to understand how habitats work is to put all your energy into investigating just one; for instance, woodlands close to your home. As well as taking photographs of the species encountered, it is a good idea to research the habitat in order to identify plants and animals and their relationships.

- Invest in books and visit websites to learn as much as you can about the relationships and interactions between the animals you are photographing and the habitats in which they live.

- Most importantly, visit your favourite environments throughout the year, recording the seasonal changes with your camera.

- While photographing wildlife in close-up may be your intent, don't forget to take some images of the animal in its habitat. This is important for depicting lifestyle. You will find such examples throughout this book.

The highest level of research is generally undertaken by photographers who have chosen to specialise in certain fields. Experts, such as "twitchers" or ornithologists (birds), entomologists (insects), and herpetologists (reptiles) become the photographer's best friend in these cases. In fact, to be able to write and illustrate a *Wild Australia Guide* in this series, a photographer may have been researching, shooting and working in the field for more than twenty years. For the average wildlife photographer, this specialised approach to photography is unappealing. Most professional wildlife photographers make images of all animal groups, mainly from an aesthetic viewpoint. Nonetheless, understanding habitats will give you an insight into how fauna lives and behaves, and ultimately, give you the best shot.

Deserts can bloom with floral abundance.

Grassland and savannas are alive with insects.

Rainforest hides many secretive species.

Coastal swamp forest and heath attracts birds.

Mountain heath is spectacular from the air.

Savanna woodland houses some macropods.

Seasonal grassland and shrubland.

Eucalypt forest is a haven for many species.

Clothing, Hides & Blinds

Constructing a hide or a blind — usually a one-sided screen to hide behind — or simply dressing in a cryptic manner, are all sensible options for wildlife photographers wanting to work unseen in the wild. If you wish to move about freely, then the colours you wear are important and should be directly determined by the colours your "targeted" animals can see and the colours of vegetation found in the particular habitat. Most animals see fewer colours than we do, but some see more! Scientists study rod or cone photo-receptors that are found in the eyes of a species to determine what colours it can see, if any. Another good indication of what an animal can see is given by the colour of its prey. Generally, duller colours can help you avoid appearing like a predator (or like prey). When in the field, I always wear muted colours, either greens or beiges. Reds, yellow or light blues (in most circumstances) are colours to avoid. Of course, if you want to take it to extremes you can always buy ex-army camouflage clothing in a disposal store. I would probably buy it myself if it were XXX-large! Boots, and possibly gaiters, are a good idea, especially in damp, squelchy "leech country" — or anywhere wet. In the north or on the coast, a supply of insect repellent is a must to stop sandflies and mosquitos from ruining your photographic adventure.

Above: Cryptically coloured clothing and slow, cautious movement combined with plenty of patience means you should be ignored by birds, reptiles and mammals.

Above: Vegetation often makes a great natural blind but a hessian structure or tent can make a good hide in open country. You may need to leave the structure erected for some time so that the birds (in this case Magpie Geese) get used to its presence.

📷 QUICK TIP

- A single sudden movement can cause all of the birds inhabiting an entire billabong to take flight, sometimes on hearing the alarm call of just one bird!

- Sounds, such as chatting or treading on dry twigs and leaves, can cause a sudden end to a photo opportunity, especially when working with macropods, which post sentries to smell, listen and watch for danger.

- Working downwind and foregoing unnatural fragrances (a great excuse for going feral), can also be important when working with mammals.

- When stalking reptiles and insects close-up, it is important to take care that your body does not cast a shadow over your quarry.

When it comes to taking photographs, there are two primary ethical issues. The first is abiding by government regulations that apply to photographing crown land such as national parks and reserves, when a permit is usually required. You will find the regulations clearly listed, however, you will need to search the individual State online and restrictions do vary. The second is one's own personal ethics, which for me are simply common sense based on the safety of the animals I am photographing. Some ethics to consider while photographing are:

COMFORT ZONE

Every species of animal has its own "comfort zone". This can be highly variable between species and also between individuals. For example, young rock-wallabies may be a lot bolder than adults. Photographers need to recognise that in most cases (at least in the wild), people are seen as a threat. The greatest skill of a talented wildlife photographer, therefore, is to learn how not to threaten their quarry.

INDUCING BEHAVIOUR

Photographing natural behaviour is always best, but your sudden presence can inadvertently cause some animals (snakes, lizards or moray eels, for instance) to rise up in a defensive posture. I would certainly take a picture in these circumstances. I work hard to interpret the body language and vocalisations of the animals I capture on film. Understanding behaviour not only gives you an insight into these animals, it also warns you if the animal is alarmed or threatened, enabling you to "back off".

BLOCKING ESCAPE

Some animals (macropods are a good example) become very stressed if their escape route is blocked. If you accidentally block the escape of some of Australia's more deadly animals, such as crocodiles and some snakes, there is every chance they will attack — possibly with fatal consequences.

FEEDING

Never feed wildlife or leave food out for animals. Habituation resulting from handouts can cause dangerous or aggressive behaviour that may lead to the death of that animal. Also, some foods are inappropriate for some species, resulting in poisoning or illness.

INTERFERING WITH ANIMALS

Many species are highly habitat-specific. A caterpillar, for example, is more valuably photographed on its host plant than on a plant it would never naturally be found on. So, unless you know your subjects well, it is best to photograph them how and where you find them.

CAPTIVE ANIMALS

Animals may be photographed in "controlled" circumstances (zoos, fauna parks or wildlife research facilities) where they are being bred or studied for one reason or another. In these circumstances, experts (many have spent a lifetime studying a particular group or species) may be able to instruct you on how to work without stressing the animals. And how to best capture a particular behaviour or activity.

Photographing Mammals

Mammals are the most alert of all the wild animals and therefore pose a great challenge to nature photographers. Like humans, other mammals learn about their surroundings by using their eyes to see, ears to hear, noses to smell, tongues to taste and skin to feel. The brain processes information and the animal reacts to meet its needs or avoid danger. For example, if a kangaroo feels hungry, it seeks grass by sight and smell, then eats it. If it sees or smells danger, it hops away. "Behaviour" is the word that describes an animal's actions, and "instinctive behaviour" is automatic and is displayed by most animals when faced with a threatening situation. For instance, a Koala will instinctively climb a tree to escape danger. "Learned behaviour" is carried out when an animal copies another animal's actions, or when (by trial and error) it discovers that an action results in a desired outcome. A young quoll learns to hunt by watching its mother hunt, and learns to defend itself by playing with its litter mates. Mammals can overcome instinctive reactions in order to survive. A wallaby may learn to tolerate humans if it becomes used to seeing them near a national park campsite, although it may remain wary elsewhere. Understanding these basics will help you interpret what is happening in photographs. An image of a kangaroo can be a portrait or it can be a study of a rarely observed behaviour that adds depth and meaning to your work.

VISITING MAMMALS

Numerous wild mammals share their habitat with humans and can be photographed in areas where they tolerate our presence. When you are travelling or camping, you can quickly build up a library of images by keeping watch after dark. At the Wallaman Falls campsite in north Queensland, for example, I photographed a Northern Brown Bandicoot and a Long-nosed Bandicoot. These are two common, but shy, small mammals, that were attracted to our campsite by the delicious smell of our evening meal — Pad Thai!

Left: The incredibly shy Black-gloved Wallaby *(35 mm DSLR, 500 mm lens, 1/250 f 5.6, ISO 320 RAW)*. **Opposite, top:** A Brush-tailed Phascogale caught on film *(23 mm SLR, 200 mm micro lens, 1/60 f 16, Velvia ISO 100, electronic flash)*.

Many Australians find that wild animals frequently visit their homes, especially when the backyard or gardens include native flora or untouched habitat. A Brush-tailed Phascogale (above) was a regular visitor to a friend's house near Kakadu National Park, where it preyed on insects attracted by the house lights. Another friend, a wildlife carer from north Queensland, had a tree-kangaroo visit her for years. It had been a hand-raised orphan that was cared for then released. Flying-foxes, possums, Koalas, bandicoots and all sorts of mammals have befriended those who have built their homes in just the right place and (wisely or by chance) left native bushland to allow the animals to keep living their natural lives. My own home in the bush just outside Brisbane is often visited by Red-necked Wallabies, Common Ringtail and Brushtail Possums and Long-nosed Bandicoots which explore my backyard or verandah.

📷 QUICK TIP

- While auto-focus does work at night, I prefer to focus manually, moving backwards or forwards to make minor adjustments to focus.

- Watch for aesthetically pleasing backgrounds that will enhance an image.

- For mammal photography, 35 mm SLR cameras are best, although compact cameras with zoom lenses and auto-focus have also been used with great success.

- For daylight work on macropods and marine mammals, I use lenses between 400 mm and 600 mm. For night work, I use the 80–200 mm zoom lens with a power flash, or sometimes two, depending on the subject.

- Apart from kangaroos, wallabies and marine mammals, most mammals are very shy and are rarely photographed in wild areas not frequented by humans. Most smaller mammals are photographed in captivity or in parks or areas where they are tolerant of, or curious about, humans. This is usually due to the likelihood of food being available.

- Small mammals — dasyurids, bandicoots, possums, bats and rodents — are nocturnal, so a head torch and a focus lantern are essential.

Kangaroos & Wallabies

The larger macropods (the Red Kangaroo and Western and Eastern Grey Kangaroos) are commonly seen in many habitats, which make acquiring good shots a relatively easy matter. However, some other wallaby species are notoriously rare and very shy, requiring stalking skills and a telephoto lens to capture them effectively on camera. Others, such as many rock-wallaby species, have limited ranges or are rare and endangered. Some, such as the Burrowing Bettong even require captive breeding programs to help safeguard their future. In these cases, special permission from a conservation authority is necessary in order to access conservation sites and take pictures. The Steve Parish *Wild Australia Guide Kangaroos & their relatives* is a useful tool for identifying species and determining their distribution and conservation status.

Once you are familiar with the species that inhabit your area, explore national park websites to discover the best spots to go and look for them, and find out what permission you might require. Most of Australia's national parks are home to some species of macropod that can be safely photographed without a permit. In some camping areas you won't need to stalk them. Wallabies (such as the Red-necked Wallaby in eastern Australia) may be so common and tame they will be stalking you, hoping for a handout! In these circumstances, you can closely study the animal's behaviour and create a series of photographs. If you talk to the ranger, you may even find out when to come back and photograph them with their pouch young.

Right: The Quokka (a small macropod found on Rottnest Island, off the WA coast near Perth), is easily approached because it has become accustomed to human activity on the island *(35 mm DSL24R, 500 mm lens, 1/500 f 5.6, ISO 320 RAW, portrait with single flash fill-in)*.

📷 QUICK TIP

- For macropod photography, 35 mm SLR cameras are preferable. This is because they provide the opportunity to use longer focal length lenses, such as 400 mm plus lenses. However, compact cameras with zoom lenses and auto focus have also been used with some success.

- Macropods do exhibit eye-shine, so if you are using a flash (either for night photography or as a fill-in flash during daylight), be sure that it is positioned so eye-shine will not be recorded.

- Watch your backgrounds. Aesthetically pleasing backgrounds will greatly enhance your images, particularly where they add a splash of colour.

Above, clockwise from top left: A female Red-necked Wallaby interacts with her yearling offspring in the early morning sunshine. Back and ring-lighting, along with the loose composition, have collectively helped create the mood of this picture *(35 mm SLR, 600 mm lens, 1/125 f 5.6, Velvia ISO 100, tripod)*; Overcast weather enabled me to capture detail on this Red-necked Wallaby and her pouch young *(35 mm SLR, 80–400 mm zoom lens, 1/125 f 5.6, Velvia ISO 100)*; Two subadult males engage in a boxing routine. The light was soft and the background uncomplicated, so the two kangaroos stand out clearly *(35 mm SLR, 80–400 mm zoom lens, 1/250 f 5.6, Velvia ISO 100)*; Because these kangaroos were some distance away, I had to grab my long telephoto lens in a hurry to make this shot, giving it a motion-like effect *(35 mm DSLR, 500 mm lens, 1/500 f 5.6, ISO 320 RAW)*.

Rock-wallabies

While there are a handful of places where rock-wallabies are rather tame (Magnetic Island and Mareeba in north Queensland and around Alice Springs in the Northern Territory, to name a few), these small, fast-moving and acutely aware macropods are a tremendous challenge to photograph. At least ten species of rock-wallaby and two wallaroo species inhabit rocky outcrops, and all are often first detected by their droppings. When you see "roo poo", it provides a good indication of where you might best do your dawn and dusk stake out. Cold nights are good, because by dawn you are likely to find rock-wallabies (either alone or in small groups) dozing in the sunshine to warm up (opposite). If you are not able to photograph a colony that is used to people, you will find that capturing these animals on film demands patience.

Above: Black-footed Rock-wallabies at Heavitree Gap, NT, approach from the rocky slopes at dawn and dusk hoping tourists will feed them prepared diet pellets supplied by the park's management. These close-up and personal opportunities, which allow portraits such as this one of a joey in the pouch, are simply not possible with a wild population that has had no interaction with humans *(35 mm DSLR, 80–400 mm zoom lens, 1/125 f5.6, ISO 320 RAW).* **Opposite, clockwise from top left:** An Allied Rock-wallaby ponders a jump on Magnetic Island, north Queensland. A zoom lens is handy for capturing such indecisive situations *(35 mm SLR, 80–400 mm zoom lens, 1/125 f8, ISO 320);* This Black-footed Rock-wallaby has come into the sunshine to warm up after a cold night. The loose framing shows the animal in its natural habitat *(35 mm SLR, 80–400 mm zoom lens, 1/250 f5.6, Velvia ISO 100);* A Black-footed Rock-wallaby with her pouch young *(35 mm DSLR, 80–400 mm zoom lens, 1/125 f8, ISO 320 RAW, flash fill-in);* The most beautifully marked of all macropods, this Yellow-footed Rock-wallaby proved a real challenge to shoot, so I used a telephoto lens fitted with a teleconverter *(35 mm SLR, 600 mm lens with 1.5 teleconverter, 1/125 f5.6, Velvia ISO 100, tripod).*

📷 QUICK TIP

- Rock-wallabies can be very timid and stress easily, so take extreme care if you approach them.
- Warm clothing, mosquito repellent, drinking water and patience are needed.
- A pair of powerful binoculars is handy for scanning the rocky outcrops.

Wombats & Koalas

Working with wombats and Koalas in the field, you can appreciate the fact these animals are distantly related. Because, although the Koala is arboreal and the wombat terrestrial, their demeanour is similar. Both are nocturnal but become active if the weather is cool and overcast, or during the early and late hours of the day. Both are also relatively easy to approach, particularly in areas where human contact is frequent. Two places where you can almost guarantee proximity to the Common Wombat are Cradle Mountain in Tasmania and Wilson's Promontory in Victoria. The delightful chocolate-brown wombat pictured below was so intent on feeding, it let me approach to within about one metre. I first encountered it while I was walking the tideline, not the normal place you'd expect to find a wombat!

Koalas, although easy to find in the wild, are not quite so easy to photograph because they prefer to reside in tall gum trees. Most of my top Koala shots are of animals that have been either hand-raised or are part of a research program and live in semi-wild conditions. There are three species of wombats and three Koala subspecies.

Left and top: Wild wombats that live close to accommodation at Cradle Mountain, Tasmania, are so used to a human presence that some individuals will continue to go about their business while you crawl around taking pictures. Under normal circumstances, however, wild wombats can be quite shy *(35 mm DSLR, 18–200 mm zoom lens, 1/30 f8, ISO 320 RAW, tripod).*

📷 QUICK TIP

- Under normal circumstances, photographs of both wombats and Koalas require lenses of a focal length of at least 400 mm. I often use a 600 mm lens.

- Digital cameras are best set to around ISO 320, with the lens set on the smallest aperture (wide open). Through selectively focusing on the animal's eye and blurring the background, you are more likely to obtain a picture where the animal stands out from its plainer background (see opposite).

- Keep sudden movement to a minimum. You may think that the animal is oblivious to your presence, but rest assured it is not.

Above: This healthy female Koala and her joey were part of a captive breeding program. I was able to spend time closely observing their behaviour as the joey learnt "Koala skills" from its mother. It was a bright, overcast day and to maintain a horizontal view I climbed another tree close by. If you shoot from the ground up with a telephoto lens, you may get little more than good shots of an animal's bottom *(35 mm SLR, 80–400 mm zoom lens, 1/125 f5.6, Velvia ISO 100)*.

Possums

Most Australians — particularly those that live close to natural bushlands, but even inner-city dwellers with balconies — are familiar with possums. At my home on Brisbane's outskirts, I have to remember to hide the fruit bowl at night. We are often visited by a community of brushtail possums (below) that can easily demolish a bowl of fruit in an evening's sitting. The primary issues regarding photographing Australian possum species are black, or very dark fur against a black background and eye-shine. Being highly curious but quite nervous creatures (especially in the wild), another difficulty is trying to record the animal's natural behaviour. Often, when capturing a pose, the possum is frozen with fear — staring wide-eyed at the camera. There is no quick resolution to this situation, other than patience and research. The only way to resolve the eye-shine is to move the flash away from a direct eye-line with the animal. The fur or background problem can be alleviated by using an additional flash unit set-up to rear-illuminate the fur, or by selecting a viewpoint that contains light-coloured vegetation behind darker areas.

Left and below: Brushtail possums, usually encountered at night, may be seen on cool, overcast days and are curious about humans. They are nimble and adept thieves of orchard fruit *(35 mm DSLR, 80–400 mm zoom lens, ISO 320 RAW, single flash, left)*.

📷 QUICK TIP

- For wild, wary possums, use an 80–400 mm zoom lens. If you want to get even closer, a zoom lens (up to 200 mm) with a single handheld flash is an ideal kit for possum photography.

- If you can, wirelessly link a second flash (or even a third) to provide the best lighting for close work. You will need an assistant (or two) to hold the flash units. Coordinating additional flashlights and focus lights can prove a bit confusing, but like most photo techniques, practice makes perfect.

Above, clockwise from top left: For a number of years, this curious Sugar Glider lived and raised litters in a hollow tree (top right) close to a friend's house south of Darwin. I used two flash units to capture it here, the main source on the left, and a modelling light on the right (set one stop less than the left flash) *(35 mm SLR, 200 mm micro lens, 1/60 f 11, Velvia ISO 100, two flash units)*; Sugar Gliders and closely related Squirrel Gliders are omnivorous and can feed rather aggressively on insects *(35 mm SLR, 200 mm micro lens, 1/60 f 11, Velvia ISO 100, one flash unit)*; Sugar Gliders photographed in a nesting box. This small community was photographed in a wildlife care facility *(35 mm DSLR, 70–180 mm micro zoom lens, 1/60 f 16, ISO 320 RAW, twin flash units)*.

Bandicoots

Although common in some areas, bandicoots (aside from the famous Bilby) are not as well known as some of Australia's other native mammals, and are often misidentified as large rats.

Generally, solitary bandicoots hide by day in little more than a shallow depression with grass pulled over the top. Their favourite food items include grubs, beetles, earthworms, berries and fungi. They are incessant diggers by night and I can hear them excavating away in my backyard or see their silhouetted forms scurrying by moonlight, through woodlands beyond my backdoor.

I have photographed bandicoots in two environments. One was of captive-bred animals and the other during instances in the wild.

I have frequently had my campsite raided by these cheeky little mammals, but far less frequently see them. If you do spot one, to obtain good photographs you will need to remain very still (they react more to movement than sound) and stay as close to the ground as possible (just slightly above the ground is best).

Above: This Long-nosed Bandicoot had become so used to humans that it simply ignored me while I took a series of behavioural photographs *(35 mm SLR, 70–180 mm zoom micro lens, 1/60 f 16, Velvia ISO 100, twin flash).*

📷 QUICK TIP

- Eye-shine is common with bandicoots, so be sure to angle your flashes so they are not in a direct line with your lens.

- While I have used 600 mm lenses with a single flash for shy, wild bandicoots, the results were flat and uninteresting. A short zoom, up to 200 or 300 mm, with twin flash units is the best kit.

- Remember to check exposures and lighting angles as you shoot with your digital camera. If depth of field is an issue, stop down by increasing the ISO.

- When photographing small mammals the size of a bandicoot, I find it is best to sit or kneel on the ground. Although, shooting even lower with a grassy foreground can create an interesting effect (see above).

Above, top to bottom: The Eastern Barred Bandicoot is a small (640 g) marsupial distinguished by pale bars or stripes on the hindquarters *(35 mm DSLR, 70–180 mm zoom micro lens, 1/60 f 16, ISO 100 RAW, twin flash)*; In a wild state, Bilbies are extremely shy. Note the poor use of twin flash units causing double shadows in the centre image; Bilbies are being captive-bred then released into large holding areas as part of a project to ensure the survival of these endangered mammals *(35 mm SLR, 70–180 mm zoom micro lens, 1/60 f 16, Velvia ISO 100, twin flashes)*.

Short-beaked Echidna

Generally shy and quick to either burrow or curl into a ball, the Short-beaked Echidna is a challenge to photograph in an appealing way. These endearing creatures exist in most habitats right across Australia. They have been seen ambling down the beach, in arid Mulga woodlands, in tropical rainforest or burrowing for grubs, larvae and worms in the cool, temperate rainforests of Tasmania. Echidnas mainly feed on ants and termites, but they will eat other invertebrates if necessary. The Tasmanian variety grows more fur due to the cold, so spikes aren't as prominent (above). As you approach these animals, which you will most likely encounter crossing the road, take care not to move suddenly or tread loudly on dried leaves or twigs. They can move quite quickly and will soon disappear into the bush. The individual above was encountered roadside in Tasmania and, no matter what I did, was entirely focused on working along the road verge in search of ants. While the individual below is a mainland variety taken at Healesville Sanctuary, Victoria.

Above: The single most important thing to watch for when photographing echidnas is that you are low enough to the ground to make your shots when the animal raises its head *(DSLR, 80–400 mm zoom lens, 1/125 f8, ISO 200 RAW)*. **Right:** You can see how the animal is nicely postured when feeding, but when ambling along can be difficult to angle so that the face and eyes are visible *(35 mm SLR, 80–400 mm zoom lens, 1/125 f5.6, Velvia ISO 100, single flash fill-in)*.

📷 QUICK TIP

- A long telephoto lens, up to 300 or 400 mm, is best for photographing echidnas. I always work with a single flash, with both flash and camera set for automatic flash fill-in.
- Depth of field (the areas in focus, from the distant point of interest to those used to frame the background) is a primary issue with framing.

Platypus

Like its monotreme relative — the Short-beaked Echidna — the unique Platypus is a difficult creature to photograph in an appealing way. In the wild, a long telephoto lens of 400 mm to 600 mm is essential. Even in areas where wild Platypuses are used to humans, you will rarely be able to shoot up close. Even if you do spot them in the wild, it is extremely difficult to photograph these mammals underwater because the water is murky. This makes aquarium displays, generally, the only way to get a good image. At Eungella National Park, Qld, I was lucky enough to take the shot below, using a 600 mm lens. Because the water's surface was well lit, I did not need to use a flash. Platypuses swim underwater with their eyes shut, so using a flash is not a problem when photographing them in aquariums. However, flashlights are not permitted in many zoos and fauna parks, so you will have to boost your digital camera's ISO rating as high as possible.

Above: A Platypus leaves its burrow to feed *(35 mm SLR, 500 mm lens, 1/250 f 5.6, Velvia ISO 100)*. **Right:** Platypus World, Tasmania, allows visitors guided walks through Platypus breeding areas *(35 mm DSLR, 70–180 mm micro zoom lens, 1/60 f 16, ISO 320 RAW, single flash)*.

📷 QUICK TIP

- A long telephoto lens is the best tool for photographing the natural behaviour of wild Platypuses. I always attach a flash as the main source or fill-in light.

- In aquariums, the best technique is to use two flashes mounted on lightweight tripods angled at 45° to eliminate glare from the glass.

- It is bad practice to interfere with these animals in any way in the wild.

Dasyurids — Predators with Pouches

Apart from the renowned Tasmanian Devil (and to a lesser extent the quolls), most Australians are largely unaware that this continent has approximately 54 other species of small, carnivorous marsupial in the order Dasyurmorphia. Most are secretive, nocturnal animals that, to the untrained eye, resemble rodents. Although some, such as the endangered Numbat (Western Australia's faunal emblem), are larger and more conspicuous. Because many species of dasyurids are rodentlike in their appearance, they are often overlooked as animals that require our care and attention in terms of protecting their habitat. They are also under considerable threat from predation by foxes and particularly feral cats. The larger better known dasyurids, like the Tasmanian Devil are dying of a contagious facial tumour disease. While, in the Top End, the Northern Quoll is at risk from eating the poisonous Cane Toad, which has encroached on its range. What does this have to do with photography? A lot! These animals desperately need to be photographed so that they are brought to the attention of the Australian public.

Above, left to right: Numbats photographed on the site of a captive-breeding and research program. The photograph on the left shows the natural behaviour of digging for termites. It took a few mornings of patient waiting before this daytime feeder was willing to emerge from its nest in a hollow log (above right) while I watched *(all photographs 35 mm SLR, 500 mm lens, 1/250 f 5.6, Velvia ISO 100)*.

📷 QUICK TIP

- Most of the smaller dasyurids in photographs have been recorded in glass terrariums and, under these circumstances, dual flashes are best. In fact, to do the job properly, a third flash used to backlight the animal is worth considering. Jiri Lochman is one photographer who has done amazing work with small mammals, dasyurids, rodents and pygmy-possums. Working with researchers, he has gone to great lengths to re-create each animal's habitat; effort which is evidenced by the great shots on his website.

Above and right: National Park campsites and picnic areas and isolated bush homes (within the ranges of one of our four species of quoll), are about the only places you are likely to "bump" into wild quolls. Active only at night, they are secretive creatures and, unless you have found a den and stake it out, the likelihood of a wild photo session is remote. Like all species and individuals, there are exceptions. The Northern Quoll, (above) was a frequent visitor to a ranger friends' bush house in the wilds of Kakadu National Park. This was no ordinary quoll. It had a liking for hot chocolate and each time we poured a cup the quoll would follow the scent and lick up any residue left in our mugs right there in the sink! So, we set-up a sandstone escarpment in the middle of the lounge room and, bingo, our quoll was right at home *(all 35 mm SLR, 500 mm lens, 1/250 f5.6, Velvia ISO 100)*.

Above, left to right: I have a fondness for Tasmanian Devils — they have great character. The work I have done with these animals been entirely in captivity. Few photographs are taken of wild Tasmanian Devils because of their secretive, solitary nature. The little wild work that has been done is generally associated with laying out baits or using traps. My work has been done in association with a conservation breeding program, where the animals are maintained in large enclosures that closely resemble parts of the Devil's natural grassy, bushland homes. Even when shooting captive animals in an artificial situation, I watch for natural postures. In the shot of the baby devil (above left), I removed eye-shine using computer software. With my software, I use the elliptical marquee tool, then go to Image/Adjustment/Replace colour, click on the eye with the spot tool, then decrease it with the light–dark tool *(all photographs 35 mm DSLR, 80–400 mm zoom lens, 1/250 f5.6, ISO 320 RAW, left picture with flash)*.

Dingoes

Unlike most other continents, Australia does not have large, native mammals in the order Carnivora. However, there is the Dingo which was introduced to the mainland some 3000 or more years ago. These shy, sometimes curious animals are at the center of a love/hate relationship with many Australians, especially in rural and outback areas. Most of my photographic encounters with Dingoes have been opportunistic and, apart from the renowned Dingoes on Fraser Island, Queensland, my chances at a shot have been limited. Nonetheless, I like to take every opportunity to make pictures, even if it is a distant animal in a large landscape.

Above: On Fraser Island, Queensland, it is comparatively easy to take good shots of the local Dingoes — some have grown bold towards humans *(35 mm SLR, 600 mm lens, 1/125 f5.6, Kodachrome ISO 64, handheld)*. **Right:** This beautiful adult Dingo lived in the heathlands behind Caloundra on the Sunshine Coast, Queensland, where it was reported to come daily to play with a domestic German Shepherd. I waited one afternoon and was lucky enough to make this single shot *(35 mm SLR, 600 mm lens, 1/125 f5.6, Kodachrome ISO 64, handheld)*.

📷 QUICK TIP

- The Dingo is one animal that requires space left around it in the frame. Firstly, to show it in its habitat, and secondly, to accentuate that it is wild.
- Use the longest telephoto lens you can muster (at least 400 mm). On Fraser Island, a shorter zoom will suffice.
- The golden rule with Dingoes is never to feed them. Wild dogs that become unafraid of humans can be dangerous around children.

Above: My most unusual encounter with a wild black Dingo was in a very isolated, infrequently visited area of the Simpson Desert way back in 1983. The animal was extremely curious. So I lay down, motionless (with my telephoto lens at the ready), and after twenty or so minutes — the animal approached to within shooting distance. I managed a few shots before it loped off into the bush *(35 mm SLR, 600 mm lens, 1/125 f5.6, Kodachrome ISO 64, handheld)*.

Up until 2006, my photographic work on Australia's flying-foxes (or bats) was limited. I had simply made records as I encountered colonies, particularly in the tropics. Fortunately (as has often been the case throughout my career), I eventually met up with two bat specialists, Dr Les Hall and Dr Graham Richards. We will be working on a major book about the biology and behaviour of Chiropterans — the mega and microbats (of which there are 86 species in Australia).

What attracted me to this group of animals was the fact that bats are not only abundant mammals, but the only ones that can fly. They also enjoy a close but little-known association with humans. While megabats are well-known and often reviled for their noisy activities in towns, microbats (both the cave and tree hollow dwellers), are little known. So, as a major, possibly never-ending project, Les and I have taken on the challenge of photographing as many species as possible. Along with their habitats and activities.

Bats' secretive nature, combined with limited close access, means these animals need to be photographed both in the wild and in captivity. The captive animals we shoot are either research animals or those that pass through wildlife care centres.

Above: Grey-headed Flying-foxes, along with Little Red, Spectacled and Black Flying-foxes are the bane of city folk in towns and cities from Melbourne to Cairns. The reason they tend to congregate noisily near cities is largely due to habitat clearing. Because these colonial animals need to roost in sites close to their food source, and orchard trees often attract them. The animals above reside in the Royal Botanic Gardens, Sydney, much to the delight of visiting tourists *(35 mm DSLR, 80–400 mm zoom lens, 1/125 f 5.6, ISO 320 RAW)*.

📷 QUICK TIP

- Apart from juveniles and some maternal females, adult flying-foxes leave their camps at night to feed. The best time to photograph flying-fox colonies is at dawn and dusk, when the animals are either leaving or returning for a day of sleeping, grooming and squabbling.

- In-flight photographs are a challenge in the low light of dawn and dusk; however, you may witness short flights around camps during the day.

Clockwise from top left: A Grey-headed Flying-fox feeding on nectar at night *(35 mm DSLR, 80–400 mm zoom lens, 1/125 f5.6, ISO 320 RAW, flashes used in front and behind)*; A captive Spectacled Flying-fox with young *(35 mm DSLR, 80–400 mm zoom lens, 1/125 f5.6, ISO 320 RAW, single flash fill has overpowered the natural light, causing a shadow. To adjust this problem, I should have adjusted the flash to lower its output by at least half an f-stop)*; A yawning mother breastfeeds her young at a bat care centre *(35 mm DSLR, 80–400 mm zoom lens, 1/125 f5.6, ISO 320 RAW, single matrix flash fill-in set on multi pattern)*; Females and young Little Red Flying-foxes *(35 mm DSLR, 750 mm lens, 1/125 f5.6, ISO 320 RAW, hard morning light causing a shadow, a fill-in flash should have been used. Bright overcast weather is best for photographing in and around flying-fox roosting sites, giving far better detail in shadowed areas)*.

Microbats

There are approximately 63 species of microbat found in Australia. Around half live in caves, while the remaining animals live in tree hollows. While the cave bats offer some ease of access, the bush bats are virtually impossible to photograph in their tree hollows in the wild. Even cave bats pose some considerable problems due to access and their high level of sensitivity. Microbats, like all small mammals, are extremely perceptive, have excellent hearing and an acute sense of smell, and therefore are easily disturbed. Over the years, Australian natural history publishing has presented the viewing public with not much more than handheld portraits of the animals. Although a few more adventurous photographers have gone to considerable lengths to photograph captive animals in-flight mainly using light-triggering devices. Others (myself included), have managed to photograph a few species in-flight, leaving cave roosts on a hit-or-miss basis by triggering the camera repeatedly in total darkness. As mentioned, I have taken on the challenge to work with Dr Les Hall to document these fascinating animals in more detail, both in the field and using captive animals (captive for research and those passing through wild care facilities). An expert in these animals, Les has been able to direct me so as to photograph not just individual animals, but photo-sequences that reveal something of the natural history.

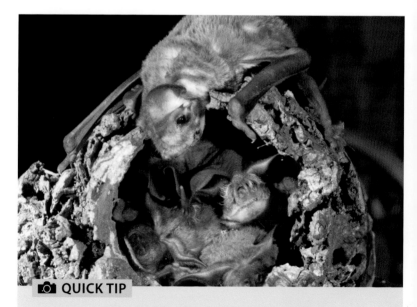

📷 QUICK TIP

- Caves, bats in-flight and hollow logs each have different requirements for equipment. A wide to medium-long zoom lens (around 8 mm to 200 mm) is a perfect lens for caves. In-flight you will need a wide lens for depth of field (I use 14 mm). Hollow logs require a micro 105 mm to 200 mm with twin macro flash units or a ring-flash. Working with an assistant is helpful, and a headlight is essential.

Opposite: This colony of Sheathtail-bats came into a wildlife centre on the Gold Coast all the way from Charleville in Central Queensland. The bats had colonised a hollow log in a wood pile that was not discovered until they arrived in Brisbane. The bats couldn't return immediately, so they were held briefly until a week or so later. The animals were surprisingly calm and went about their normal "who gets the best spot inside the log" behaviour while I made a series of photographs. I find these sorts of story sequences particularly valuable *(35 mm DSLR, 70–180 mm micro zoom lens, 1/125 f 16, ISO 320 RAW, twin macro flash).* **Top, left:** One of a colony of Leafnosed-bats that inhabited an abandoned mine shaft. By remaining still for some time I have found that some species of microbats will quieten to the extent that they will go about their business (usually sleeping by day) and ignore the flashlight completely *(35 mm DSLR, 70–180 mm micro zoom lens, 1/125 f 16, ISO 320 RAW, twin macro flash).* **Bottom, left:** These Little Bent-wing Bats are mainly juveniles and adult females. Having been fed at their roosting site deep inside the cave by their mothers, it is now time for the juveniles to venture out. They depart approximately 30 minutes after sundown. To capture a photograph of bats leaving roosts I use an infrared triggered camera with two or three wireless controlled flashlights, depending on the cave structures. So as to not unduly disturb the bats, I triggered only three or four times in one sitting, then waited five minutes, before triggering again. I have been reasonably fortunate to create some successful pictures due to the large number of bats in some cases. A light-trigger device would be essential for flight photographs when bat numbers are lower or at cave sites where only small numbers reside *(35 mm DSLR, 14 mm lens, 1/60 f 22, ISO 600 RAW, twin flashlights).*

Rodents — Rats & Mice

Apart from the research workers who create photographic records (which is often a frightened animal in the bottom of a bucket), few wildlife photographers spend much of their time photographing rodents. This is a pity really, because these are endearing creatures with fascinating natural histories. Much like the smaller dasyurids, these shy and elusive animals are entirely nocturnal and extremely wary. They have reason to be on guard. They are the primary diet for many snakes and nocturnal birds. I have had little good fortune with wild rodents — my growing collection is comprised of captive research and exhibition animals.

Left: A researcher checks her fence trap in western NSW. This is a typical set-up for checking which species inhabit an area. If you have contacts you can go along as a helper on these trips and take your pictures in small field pens prior to release *(35 mm DSLR, 24 mm lens, 1/125 f 11, ISO 320 RAW).* **Below:** This Rock-rat was photographed in a display terrarium *(35 mm DSLR, 70–180 mm micro zoom lens, 1/125 f 16, ISO 320 RAW, single electronic flash).*

📷 QUICK TIP

- Similarly to microbats and also applicable to dasyurids, it is possible to photograph wild rodents using light-sensitive triggering devices. The principle is having either a known den entrance or a runway frequented by a known species so that you can set-up the equipment.

- A macro lens between 80 mm and 200 mm and a twin macro flash unit is ideal. A third mobile wire flash is excellent for backlighting when the opportunity arises.

Top and above: Three of us were "frogging" in a rainforest, chatting away and not concerned about our noise level, when this delightful melomys was spotted sitting on an open palm frond chewing on a nut. We all took pictures, starting from a distance, then working closer and closer for a nice portrait. We were lucky. A rodent would normally have disappeared due to the noise we were making *(35 mm DSLR, 70–180 mm micro zoom lens, 1/125 f 16, ISO 320 RAW, twin macro flash)*. **Left:** This curious Water-rat was photographed in a large display terrarium *(35 mm DSLR, 70–180 mm micro zoom lens, 1/125 f 16, ISO 320 RAW, single electronic flash)*.

Photographing Reptiles

It is not only Australians who are interested in Australian reptiles — nature lovers from all over the world are fascinated by our country's abundance of reptile species. Particularly, those popularised by the media — the snakes, goannas, crocodiles and turtles. Dramatic animals like these understandably attract attention, but the many smaller reptiles, such as geckoes, dragons and skinks are also extremely appealing as subjects for photography. Some reptiles, the dragons in particular, have a sinister look about them and conjure up thoughts of the children's storybook world of mythical fire-breathing dragons from medieval times.

The majority of reptile photographers are primarily intent on photographing the animals as records of the species in their natural habitat, side on and with a good angle to see the features that designate their identification. This work is time consuming and may not allow one to become involved in photographing the species' various behaviours. Aspects such as feeding, defensive postures, courting, mating, colour variations between males and females, and even variations in colour throughout a species distribution all provide opportunities for photographic sequences. Personally, I am more interested in photo essays; images through which a story can be told.

Then there is an additional challenge, as there is with all animals, in not just recording these animals physically, but also portraying them in a way that evokes emotion. Remember to adhere to ethical work practices. This is where your artistic skills come into play — the textures, the angle of light, the angle of view and so on.

Opposite: This Green Tree Python was captive bred under permit, however it was re-introduced to the wild for photographic purposes *(35 mm SLR, 200 mm micro lens, 1/60 f 16, Velvia ISO 100, single flash)*.

📷 QUICK TIP

- A 35 mm SLR digital camera is best for reptile photography, preferably with a motor drive and automatic metering system.

- Because reptiles range in size from tiny geckoes to giant crocodiles there are no ideal lenses. The full range of focal lengths will be useful. For the majority of small skinks, geckoes, dragons, and even snakes, a 70–180 mm micro zoom lens is ideal. For full-length non-venomous snakes, I would choose a moderately wide-angle lens, such as 35 mm. Zoom lenses may be easier because you can move from a full body shot to a portrait with a flip of the wrist. If you meet a venomous snake in the wild, give it a wide berth and use a 200 mm lens — it's easier and safer.

- Reptiles, being cold blooded, are more likely to be active when it's warm, day or night. On warm nights, I recommend you carry a powerful electronic flash with automatic flash-fill.

- If you wish to photograph reptiles, I strongly advise you to do your research, particularly regarding habitat. Reptiles are usually secretive and, being cryptically coloured, are not easy to find in the wild.

Monitors, Dragons & Skinks

At times, it is important for the photographer to work at ground level. However, because this group of reptiles are fast moving, generally small in size (particularly the skinks) and live in a world where small obstructions — grasses, rocks, leaf litter — can easily spoil a photograph, zoom micro lenses and short wide zooms should be considered. You will find that physical movement (on your part), such as changing your lenses or viewpoint, will disturb your quarry. An alternative is to use a low stool, a long lens possibly fitted with an extension tube to enable close focus, and a tripod. This way you can "keep your distance" and record natural behaviour.

Left: There is much behaviour that can be photographed when working with Lace Monitors. Their tree-climbing ability is just one of many traits *(35 mm DSLR, 24 mm lens, 1/125 f 16, ISO 320 RAW)*. **Above:** Generally, a large Sand Monitor like this would quickly scamper into the bush when approached. I was able to follow this individual for some time, photographing it hunting *(35 mm SLR, 80–200 mm zoom lens, 1/125 f 16, Kodachrome ISO 64)*.

📷 QUICK TIP

- If you are serious about photographing this group of animals, I highly recommend that you start by working long and hard with an individual species. Try and acquire as many varied photographs of its behaviour as possible. Behaviour-like defence, courting, mating, egg laying, the young breaking free from nests and eggs, and feeding can all be a focus. This project will then remain with you as a guide while you work with other species.

Above: This picture of the Thorny Devil is an example of how a long lens and a short, managed depth of field, clean background, low to the ground perspective and loose composition can heighten the drama of a reptile photograph *(35 mm SLR, 200 mm micro lens, 1/250 f 5.6, Kodachrome ISO 64).* **Right:** An example of how front and backlighting can bring a dark animal in a dark environment to life *(35 mm SLR, 105 mm micro lens, 1/125 f 16, Kodachrome ISO 64. The camera was mounted on a tripod, focused on the animal. The front flash was attached to the hot shoe on the camera and the second flash was held behind the animal).* **Bottom right:** Encountered asleep on a log, this Frilled Lizard was quick to adopt a defensive posture when I approached it *(35 mm SLR, 80–400 mm zoom lens, 1/125 f 16, ISO 320, single flash fill-in).*

Above: Male Eastern Water Dragons, like most dragons, assume vivid colours when courting females, making for a great picture *(clockwise from left: 35 mm DSLR, 80–400 mm zoom lens, 1/125 f 16, ISO 320 RAW, single flash fill-in; 35 mm SLR, 80-400 mm zoom lens, 1/60 f 8, Velvia ISO 100, single flash fill-in; 35 mm SLR, 80-400 mm zoom lens, 1/125 f 16, Velvia ISO 100, single flash fill-in).*

Geckoes

To locate geckoes, wear a headlamp so that the angle of the beam of light is directly parallel with your line of sight. You will see eye-shine as the torchlight reflects in the animal's eyes. Often, the animal will freeze, allowing you time to close in and focus your lens. Unless unduly alarmed, geckoes will often remain stationary for some time. Then, if you want natural behaviour, it is best to back off using the edge of your light, or another softer light. Due to the fact that they are often colourful and well known to visit houses, these curious little animals are popular in the world of reptiles. Kids too, find them appealing, maybe because they have a similar look to Steven Spielberg's movie character ET.

Above: These three photographic approaches to a Smooth Knob-tailed Gecko, along with the photographs opposite, illustrate just how many approaches can be made. If you want to sell your images or tell a story with them, it is important to vary your approaches. Note top right, I have moved my single flash around in front, creating an effect that suggests the animal is out and about in the dark leaving an overhang, possibly a hollow log. The main picture takes a particularly appealing perspective, head on, while the picture bottom right is a downward view, which is excellent for etching in a field guide identifying the species *(35 mm SLR, 200 mm micro lens, 1/125 f 16, Kodachrome ISO 64, single flash)*.

📷 QUICK TIP

- Even if your house gecko is a feral Asian House Gecko, you can always practice your skills photographing them.

- Don't be surprised if the gecko you are photographing utters a "chk-chk-chk" clicking sound — geckoes are some of the few reptiles that utter sound.

- The best kit? A zoom micro, 70–180 mm micro and macro twin flashes.

Above: I detected this cryptically coloured Leaf-tailed Gecko at night as a result of its eye-shine. By wearing a camping headlamp, it is possible to detect the eye-shine of geckoes from many metres. This is by far the easiest way to find these elusive animals *(35 mm SLR, 200 mm micro lens, 1/125 f 16, Kodachrome ISO 64, single flash)*.

Left: Etched from its background, the intricate patterning is better appreciated.

Above: Only geckoes and legless lizards clean their eyes with their tongue. A transparent scale covers and protects the eye from damage. This is an interesting behaviour to photograph. This beautifully marked Velvet Gecko visited our campsite in the Pilbara, WA *(35 mm SLR, 200 mm micro lens, 1/125 f 16, Kodachrome ISO 64, single flash)*.

Above: The Eastern Prickly Knob-tailed Gecko, like its relatives, is active at night searching for spiders and insects. During the heat of the day it will retreat into crevices *(35 mm SLR, 200 mm micro lens, 1/125 f 16, Kodachrome ISO 64, single flash)*.

Snakes

Snakes may react to a flash or the sound of a motor drive. Any sudden movements can cause defensive and even aggressive behaviour. If you add to this a deliberate high level of antagonistic behaviour on your part — taunting the snake to cause it to rise up, or unnecessarily handling the animal — it may strike. Many snake experts will admit that they have come close to death due to a snakebite, so take care. Emulating the "wrangling" you see on TV does not advance snake appreciation among the public. It simply perpetuates the existing fear people already have of these fascinating creatures.

If any animal requires a series of images to tell its story, it is the snake. The primary reason for this is that because they are long and thin, it is a challenge to make photographs that capture head detail and the creature's full body length. Especially when the animal moves and is drawn out to its full length.

Above, left: Yellow when juvenile, the Green Tree Python is considered Australia's most striking species. Their range is restricted to the Iron Range rainforest in Far North Qld. This animal was placed in a rainforest setting for photography *(35 mm SLR, 200 mm micro lens, 1/60 f 16, Velvia ISO 100, single flash)*. **Above, right:** This Carpet Snake lives in my backyard and is extremely curious — pythons will strike and bite if harassed but are not dangerous to humans *(35 mm SLR, 200 mm micro lens, 1/60 f 16, Velvia ISO 100, single flash)*.

📷 QUICK TIP

- I always try and photograph each snake as a vertical full body shot, preferably in the open and without any obstructions where possible. This is for etching — see image opposite. I also record the animal merged into its habitat and follow this with a portrait at low level showing the tongue.

- The lens rig for snakes is similar to that suggested for dragons. I would add to my kit solid leather boots, possibly leggings or gaiters. If you're intending to photograph a dangerous species, or a species that you are unsure of, use a telephoto lens and try not to antagonise the animal.

Above: The Tiger Snake is common within its range — active by day and at night when frogs are abundant. They vary in colour, so there are many different ways to capture this highly venomous snake (with several fatalities to its credit) on film. These snakes were photographed on commission and I had the handler present. Such snakes are capable of making a lethal bite *(35 mm SLR, 200 mm micro lens, 1/60 f 16, Velvia ISO 100, single flash).*

Left and right: A portrait of a Tiger Snake and a vertical taken from above for etching. These are two angles that I always try to make as I encounter new species *(35 mm SLR, 200 mm micro lens, 1/60 f 16, Velvia ISO 100, single flash).*

POTENTIALLY LETHAL SNAKES

Most people that want to trek into the Australian bush are nervous about encountering dangerous snakes. To be cautious is wise. These animals are very well camouflaged and when they're lying motionless, warming themselves in the sun, you might not always be aware of their presence. Some, such as death adders, are nocturnal, while others such as copperheads, are active both day and night. However, in most circumstances the snake will detect your presence and be long gone. Australia has 75 of the world's 210 or more species of elapids, or front-fanged snakes, and of these more than twenty are potentially dangerous to humans. Most prefer to retreat rather than bite, but all will strike if harassed. The Inland Taipan is Australia's most venomous snake, but that does not make it Australia's most dangerous snake. Judged by the number of snakebite deaths, that title goes to the Eastern Brown Snake. Unless you know these animals intimately, you are best to simply give them their space. My own work with dangerous snakes has mostly been done with snake experts.

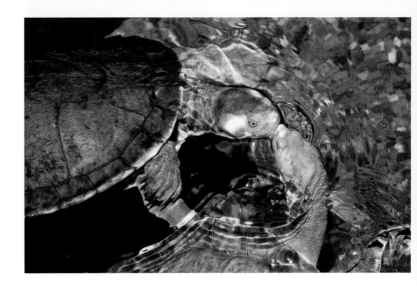

There are 33 species of freshwater turtle in Australia. All bar one species belong to a group known as the cheluids, or side-necked turtles, that withdraw their head by folding it to the side of their carapace. Members of this group are confined to Australasia and South America and are further categorised by having either short or long necks. The short-necked turtles are primarily vegetarian while the long-necks are carnivorous, using their long necks to strike at prey. The exception is the Pig-nosed Turtle, which belongs to a group of animals known as the cryptodires turtles, which withdraw their head directly back into their shell. Like their marine cousins, freshwater turtles lay eggs on land.

This popular group of animals is an excellent group to focus your attention on if you are a budding naturalist photographer. Although often fairly secretive in the wild, there are some species that are quite common, and they are generally well represented along the east coast in the ponds of botanical gardens.

Top: If you are lucky enough to encounter turtles during the courting and breeding season, you will find more action to shoot than normally encountered. These Eastern Long-necked Turtles were courting and extremely active *(photographed in an enclosed waterhole, 35 mm DSLR, 80–200 mm zoom lens, 1/60 f 13, ISO 250 RAW, single flash)*.

📷 QUICK TIP

- A long zoom lens up to 300 mm or even 400 mm would be ideal so that you can vary your focal length as you move closer.

- If you do see turtles in areas frequented by people, you will probably find that they will go about their business quite boldly. In other areas, they may be more sensitive and simply vanish into the murky depths at the crack of a twig.

Above and right: Hatchling turtles make for appealing shots, especially the Saw-shelled Turtle. This delightful little individual was photographed in a freshwater aquarium *(both images 35 mm DSLR, 70–180 mm micro zoom lens, 1/125 f 22, ISO 320 RAW, single flash).*

Top, left to right: Adult Saw-shelled Turtle on the surface and a Cann's Long-necked Turtle sunning on a log — two activities relatively easy to capture on film with most turtle species *(both images 35 mm DSLR, 80–200 mm zoom lens, 1/125 f 11, ISO 320 RAW).* **Above:** There are occasions, just as in the case of this of a Pig-nosed Turtle, where actually photographing them underwater in their habitat is possible. This is particularly the case in the tropics where the clarity in freshwater streams and rock holes can be exceptional *(35 mm rangefinder amphibious cameras, 15 mm lens, 1/30 f 16, Kodachrome ISO 64, 2 metres underwater).*

Crocodiles

Capturing crocodile behaviour via the camera is a very time-consuming project. These animals are extremely efficient carnivores, perfectly adapted to their environment, and well camouflaged. I recall a boat trip with crocodile researchers working on the Alligator River in Kakadu some years back. The researchers had taken with them (to act as a spotter) an old Aboriginal man who had spent his whole life living in saltwater and freshwater crocodile country. I was astounded at how many he spotted, most of which would have passed unseen by the rest of us. The Estuarine Crocodile is dangerous to humans, seeing us merely as a potential source of food. Unless you wish to devote many years of study, you will have to be content with taking photographs as you pass by in a boat. There, exciting images are still possible of these prehistoric creatures as they remain on the bank, or as they are rushing into the water when disturbed. Their hunting, incredible nest-building and maternal behaviour are subjects that have not, to my knowledge, been well documented with still cameras in Australia. While the Freshwater Crocodile is similar in many of its behaviours, they are not known to attack humans and, like the Estuarine Crocodile, are not well photographed. I recommend using lenses between 300 mm and 600 mm to photograph wild crocodiles.

Above: The calm, reflective waters of a crocodile farm can be a great place to start taking your crocodile photographs. There are many in the Top End around Darwin, and in the north-east around Cairns *(35 mm SLR, 400 mm lens, 1/125 f 16, Velvia ISO 100)*.

📷 QUICK TIP

- To photograph wild crocodiles, lenses between 300 mm and 600 mm are best.
- You may need to sit and watch for lengthy periods if you are looking for interesting behaviour — unless they are feeding, crocodiles are generally inactive, especially when "sunbaking".

Above and left: Quietly drifting in a boat, preferably alone or with quiet company, is a great way to get some moody shots of crocodiles. These three photographs illustrate how the lighting and atmospheric conditions are also part of the ingredients that make effective pictures. Like all wild animal photography, be patient. The animal may do nothing more than drift for some time, however if you can stand the mossies biting you, wait it out — there is bound to be action eventually *(all with 35 mm SLR, 80–400 mm lenses, Velvia ISO 100)*.

Photographing Amphibians

A frog is an amphibian, which means it can live two ways — in water and on land. A frog has moist, soft skin that may act as a breathing organ, and its skin is fragile and very sensitive to touch. Many species, if handled, may also change their colour. So it is best not to handle these animals during photographic sessions.

Typically, frogs' eggs do not have hard shells, and are laid in water or in damp places. The tadpole (one of which hatches from each egg), has a tail, is limbless, is mainly vegetarian and breathes through gills. As it matures, it grows limbs, absorbs its tail, loses its gills, and develops lungs. It undergoes metamorphosis into an air-breathing, land-living, tailless adult that eats small animals. Frogs are amazing subjects for sequential photo-storytelling.

Opposite, clockwise from top: A tiny male Wallum Sedge-frog *(35 mm DSLR, 70–180 mm micro zoom lens, 1/60 f32, ISO 320, RAW, twin micro flashes)*; Graceful Tree-frogs can usually be easily approached while mating *(35 mm DSLR, 70–180 mm micro zoom lens, 1/60 f32, ISO 320 RAW, twin micro flashes)*; Sometimes a frog like this Graceful Tree-frog will be found sitting in just the right spot *(35 mm DSLR, 70–180 mm micro zoom lens, 1/60 f32, ISO 320 RAW, twin micro flashes)*.

📷 QUICK TIP

- A continuous light on frogs' eyes will cause them to close the iris and the black pupil will appear as an unappealing slit. If you see the pupils closing during a shoot, remove the focus light and let the animal rest.

- Frogs live in specific habitats, so be careful if you want to move them to a different habitat to take photographs, in fact, best not to move them at all.

- Learn as much as you can about frogs in general and find out which frogs occur in your area.

- If you are developing land, do your best to preserve frog habitat. Don't drain frog breeding sites.

- Make your garden frog-friendly, with damp, shady places. A backyard pond will attract frogs.

- Why not raise suitable frogs for your area? Stock your pond with locally caught tadpoles — don't introduce strangers from other areas.

- Remember that for frogs to exist, tadpoles need to be left in peace.

- Don't use pesticides or herbicides if there is any other way of controlling a pest, animal or plant.

- Discourage domestic pets from damaging or killing frogs.

- Frogs are protected by law in Australian States and it is illegal to capture and move them without State-issued permits.

- Handling frogs during photographic shoots can damage their skin and a harassed frog will make an unappealing photograph (not to mention the ethics of knowingly harming the animal). Some have poisonous exudations.

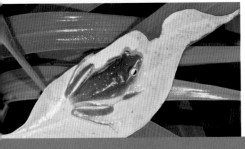

Ground & Tree-frogs

There are more than 200 species of frog found in Australia. Many of these animals are in danger as they are very sensitive to pollution, habitat destruction and predation from introduced pests, such as the Cane Toad.

Frogs live in a wide variety of habitats. There are those that live in trees and others that live in leaf litter or freshwater swamps — yet others live in alpine conditions and some in the aridlands. They are nocturnal so you will need a miner's lamp to detect eye-shine. Generally, frogs are more approachable than reptiles and may remain quite motionless while you take your photographs. However, as with most wildlife photography, it is more likely that you will have to be the one remaining motionless if you are after behavioural shots, such as frogs eating, burrowing or hopping.

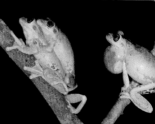

Top, right: This Graceful Tree-frog is transforming from a tadpole into a frog *(35 mm DSLR, 70–180 mm micro zoom lens, 1/60 f 32, ISO 320 RAW, twin micro flashes).* **Centre, right:** Laughing Tree-frogs at the peak of the breeding season are very easy to approach *(35 mm DSLR, 70–180 mm micro zoom lens, 1/60 f 32, ISO 320 RAW, twin micro flashes).* **Bottom, right:** This Great Barred Frog was photographed swimming in an artificial pond *(35 mm DSLR, 70–180 mm micro zoom lens, 1/60 f 32, ISO 320 RAW, twin micro flashes).* **Opposite:** These Striped Rocket-frog photographs illustrate the angles I always try and capture with each frog species I encounter. The top image is a dorsal view and the bottom one a side view *(35 mm DSLR, 70–180 mm micro zoom lens, 1/60 f 32, ISO 320 RAW, twin micro flashes).*

📷 QUICK TIP

- 35 mm SLR cameras are best for frog photography, preferably with a motor drive and automatic metering system, although the latter is not essential.

- Because they are small animals, use a macro lens, preferably 105 mm or (even better still), a 200 mm macro lens.

- Most frog encounters will be made at night so I recommend using a powerful electronic flash with a system that provides automatic flash-fill.

Photographing Birds

There is no doubt that birds provide a challenge for photographers. They are very wary creatures, quickly responding to even the slightest hint of danger and certainly not content to sit still and patiently wait for you to set-up and take your photograph. All species, particularly solitary individuals, will have their comfort zone. In the case of flocking birds, you have many sets of ears and eyes on guard. Whatever the species, you will need to immerse yourself (body, mind and spirit) in the bird's natural environment. So, whether that environment is mud flats, the biting insect world of mangrove or freshwater paperback swamps, or aridland scrub — wherever a species calls home — you will need to get in there and become part of that environment.

Apart from the owls and some birds-of-prey, birds are active during the day. Many are particularly active during the early and late hours or when food is more readily available.

The most important tools for photographing birds are telephoto lenses with focal lengths of between 300 mm and 600 mm. I think that moderate to advanced camera skills are essential because most species, other than Black Swans, common ducks and friendly Pelicans, will not provide a great deal of time for decision making. Lenses longer than 400 mm may require a tripod or monopod for support, although I have made many images with a handheld camera, usually because light availability dictates a higher shutter speed. In today's world of variable ISO ratings and the ability to manage digital noise levels, the opportunities for handheld photography with longer lenses has grown.

📷 QUICK TIP

- A 35 mm SLR is the best camera for bird photography, preferably with a motor drive and automatic metering system, but the latter two are not essential.

- Lenses from 300 mm to 600 mm are ideal. I use 300 mm and a 80–400 mm zoom lens for close work with small bush birds in and among shrubs, with an automatic flash for fill-in if necessary. Water and sea birds are better tackled with a 500 mm or 600 mm lens, and you may even choose to use a tele-converter.

- A tripod or monopod will be essential, especially in low light when a slow shutter speed is required.

- You will need to be patient and calm. Any anxiety or noise will cause your highly sensitive and acutely aware quarry to take flight.

- As with all subjects, the foreground and background are almost as important as the primary subject. A little computer editing might prove necessary, at a later date, to remove ugly and intrusive elements.

Above: Urban parks, reserves, wildlife sanctuaries, national parks, picnic and camping areas, roadside stops, and botanical gardens in Australia provide great opportunities to develop your bird photography skills. You will find in these areas that a bird's comfort zone will be far greater than would normally be the case away from these areas. You may even find, as I did in the situation above, that the birds are too close for comfort *(the camera is an SLR with a 500 mm lens)*.

Other camera aids I recommend are automatic focus and through-the-lens automatic metering. Both assist in getting shots away a lot quicker. A motor drive, now an integral part of most high quality cameras, gives you another advantage over an animal capable of moving with alarming speed. Particularly if, like small bush birds, they give no warning that flight is imminent. Larger birds, such as birds-of-prey, water birds, and so on, will engage in all sorts of pre-flight body language so you are far more likely to have the time to compose and fine-focus before take-off.

In this book, I have grouped the birds according to a general approach you could follow. The overall photographic style, however, can be applied to any group. The groupings relate more to a combination of habitat and general behaviour than to taxonomic groups. For example, sea birds are used to being in an open environment and may not take flight until you have crossed the invisible line that defines their comfort zone. In the closed environment of a small bush bird, the comfort zone, into which intrusion will not be tolerated, will be much smaller but it may still encompass most of the area available to you.

Bird photography, for all its challenges and frustrations, can be richly rewarding. The feeling of elation when an image turns out the way you imagined is indescribable. When you see the result you were after, you know that you have captured on film one of nature's most elusive beauties through your skill, nous and determination.

Above: One of my favourite waterbird photographs, a Jacana from the tropical Top End. It captures all the elements — movement, reflection, silhouette and mood *(35 mm SLR, 500 mm lens, 1/250 f 5.6, Kodachrome ISO 64).*

"Waterbirds" is the collective name for birds whose principal habitat is freshwater lakes, rivers, floodplains and coastal estuarine waterways. This large group of birds includes well-known species such as ducks, geese, herons, stilts and the ever-popular photographic subject, the Australian Pelican. What makes these birds so special to photograph is the component of water in the composition. Water offers reflections, patterns and textures, and (depending on the sky colours) some delightful colour tones that can enhance your images. Some, such as the egrets, the Brolga and the Jabiru, are very elegant, and the preening and courting postures they assume can be very appealing.

This is a wonderful group of birds with which to develop bird photography skills. You will find many of the urban lakes and waterways have relatively approachable residents. The light is warmest in the early morning or evening, and I use lenses from 400 mm to 600 mm.

📷 QUICK TIP

- Waterbirds, if disturbed during nesting, may desert their chicks. If there are marauding gulls around, stay well away as they will attack and kill chicks left unguarded.

- Waterbirds in colonies or groups do have a collective comfort zone and if you infringe upon it, all the birds will take flight at the first cries of alarm.

- A long lens mounted on a tripod will also allow you to sit quietly watching and waiting for an unusual preening posture, or maybe an interaction between two species. A small collapsible lightweight seat is handy for this sort of work.

Top: Here is a classic example of how very beautiful photographs can be made in a wildlife sanctuary like Healesville in Victoria. The large waterbird display has numerous species that are not only rare and endangered, but also quite difficult to approach during the breeding season. I run photo workshops for kids periodically in such wildlife sanctuaries and find all of the "in the wild" challenges can still be experienced *(35 mm DSLR, 80–400 mm zoom lens, 1/250 f 11, ISO 320 RAW, handheld).* **Above:** These courting Black Swans offer a reverse metering challenge to the image above. The white birds above needed to be spot metered, the black birds multi-pattern metered *(35 mm DSLR, 80–400 mm zoom lens, 1/250 f 11, ISO 320 RAW, handheld).*

Groundbirds

While some groundbirds are incapable of flight (the cassowary and Emu being two), other members of this group will only fly when escaping predators or roosting in trees. Birds that are in this category include quail, the Australian Brush-turkey, Australian Bustard, Orange-footed Scrubfowl and rails. The majority of these birds are cryptically coloured and habitat-specific and most are not commonly seen. On the other hand, others are commonly seen in urban areas (such as the brush-turkeys), which have adopted Brisbane's western suburbs as their homes. They start building their giant incubation mounds in suburban gardens without giving consideration to the often-fastidious labour that the householder has put in. I have several making themselves at home on my block and apart from them teasing the dog, I enjoy sharing my world with them. Even cassowaries wander into the odd northern Queensland backyard where their tropical rainforest home still remains. All these birds pose interesting photographic challenges. Emus are well known to people who travel the back blocks of Australia, even playing "chicken" with fast moving cars!

Above: The Malleefowl can be both extremely shy or (if you are fortunate) may even completely ignore you. This mound-building male had a comfort zone of about 15 metres *(35 mm SLR, 500 mm lens, 1/125 f8, Velvia ISO 100, tripod).*

Above: Distributed from northern NSW to northern Qld, the Australian Brush-turkey is often seen roaming national park camping and picnic areas in search of food. Like other megapodes, they have an interesting life history to photograph *(SLR, 80–400 mm zoom lens, 1/126 f5.6, ISO 320 RAW).*

📷 QUICK TIP

- Careful stalking is usually required when photographing these birds. They do have a habit of walking either directly to you or on an angle away from you on approach. One way to overcome this problem is to circle the bird, then sit quietly, trusting it will reappear at an angle that is more appealing.

- With some care not to disturb, a hide on a mound or nest can produce good results.

- An 80–200 mm, or better still an 80–400 mm zoom lens, is ideal for photographing most megapodes, especially the larger species.

Above: It is always exciting when you encounter a megapode with chicks. This Emu took me on a merry walk as I tried to get a clear shot of dad with his brood.

ARE YOU SPEEDING ?

Left: The unique and beautiful Southern Cassowary is found in the tropical rainforests of north Queensland, the Daintree and Mission Beach in particular. While some individuals can be bold, most are extremely shy. This species poses an excellent and important challenge to photograph. All megapode males build the mounds, taking particular care in ensuring the temperature is kept at a consistent 32–34 °C (SLR, 80–200 mm zoom lens, 1/126 f 5.6, Kodachrome ISO 64).

Sea & Shore Birds

Terns, gannets, frigatebirds, tropicbirds and noddies have one thing in common — they have amazing fishing skills. Each species has adapted to survive in one of the harshest environments on Earth. Great Barrier Reef coral cays are ideal locations to work with these fishers, especially one of those with resort accommodation, such as Heron and Lady Elliot Islands. Both these islands have large colonies of permanent sea bird residents that have become relatively tolerant of people and will go about their business taking little notice of you. Many nest right outside your door, so if you are looking for a quiet break (especially during the breeding season) these islands are not for you. In some remote island areas, signs have been erected to stop people entering and disturbing the larger, more sensitive colonies. There is no need to enter a colony physically as you can do that with a long telephoto lens.

Above: Taking flight, courting, bathing, colonial nest and chick care — just four of the many great aspects of a Crested Tern's fascinating behaviour *(all 35 mm SLR, 80–400 mm zoom lens, Kodachrome ISO 64).*

📷 QUICK TIP

- Sea birds are abundant residents of the coastal environment. It is important not to disturb these animals during their nesting season because, if you scare away the parent birds, you may endanger the chicks or the eggs by leaving them open to predators. Give rookeries a wide berth, observe and photograph them from a safe distance.

- Two ways to approach sea birds are — walk and shoot and sit and shoot. I usually consider both possibilities, with a 500–600 mm lens tripod-mounted resting on one shoulder and a 80–400 mm zoom hanging on the other.

Top: Sea and shore birds coming and going, roosting, preening or feeding while silhouetted against reflecting sky colours can make effective images. You will need wet sand or mud as the mirror *(35 mm SLR, 80–400 mm zoom lens, 1/125 f 16, Velvia ISO 100, handheld)*. **Centre, left:** Brown Boobies roosting against a vermilion sky. Island photography, particularly those islands with low vegetation, do offer many opportunities for interesting effects, particularly during the periods of sunrise and sunset *(35 mm SLR, 600 mm lens, 1/125 f 5.6, Velvia ISO 100)*. **Centre, right:** Shore birds, the majority of species being migratory, can be another challenge due to the fact that most form large nervous flocks. When roosting or feeding as a flock they usually have a large area as their comfort zone which requires long telephoto lenses, often with tele-converters *(35 mm SLR, 80–400 mm zoom lens, 1/500 f 8, Velvia ISO 100, tripod)*. **Above, left:** A Roseate Tern is seen here hovering almost motionlessly into the wind. In these circumstances, in-flight photography is relatively easy. A white bird on a dark background is best metered using central weight *(35 mm SLR, 80–400 mm zoom lens, 1/500 f 8, Velvia ISO 100, handheld)*. **Above, right:** Masked Boobies, unlike most sea bird species, may have a comfort zone as little as a few metres, even when caring for a chick. All gannets nest in colonies *(35 mm SLR, 80–400 mm zoom lens, 1/125 f 16, Velvia ISO 100, handheld)*.

Perching Birds

Perching birds, such as the fairy-wrens, finches and honeyeaters, represent the majority of Australian species and many are the most difficult to photograph. In this area of interest, your spontaneous reactions will be tested to the limit (as will your skills as a hunter), because perching birds are extremely aware of their surroundings. In most instances they will be alert to your presence long before you spot them. The reason for their sensitivity is that the smaller birds must be constantly on the watch for predators. On guard against other birds or reptiles, the latter is a particular threat when the birds are nesting and raising young.

To photograph small birds I employ three approaches. One is to walk, equipped with 300 mm to 400 mm lenses. This can be particularly productive if I am in and around flowering shrubs. A busily feeding bird is often easier to approach. Another method is to stand, usually near a large flowering shrub that appears to attract smaller birds, with a longer lens, around 500 mm or 600 mm. The third approach is to use a blind, but I generally use vegetation rather than rig a structure.

Below: A 400 mm plus telephoto, even short at times, is the lens to use for the delightful Rainbow Bee-eater. This back-to-back pair were intently watching for insects *(35 mm SLR, 600 mm lens, 1/250 f8, Velvia ISO 100, tripod).*

Below: Alert and agile, the Lemon-breasted Fly Catcher is a fine example of a bird that returns to the same roosting perch, between short forays for prey *(35 mm DSLR, 80–400 mm zoom lens, 1/125 f11, ISO 320 RAW, handheld).*

📷 QUICK TIP

- When small birds are nesting, they will search for food in the immediate region of their nest and often perch on the same branches as they move through their territory. If you don't get a shot first time round, be patient and you may get a second chance.

- Small perching birds, in particular, are very sensitive around their nesting areas and may desert their chicks if disturbed. I tend to concentrate on their many other fascinating behaviours and keep away from nests. If nesting birds are your objective, work from a hide or blind and find out as much as you can about the bird's behaviour before you start.

Top: If your camera offers variable focusing options, I suggest that you use a single focus point when shooting around vegetation. This then enables you to perform selective spot focus thereby eliminating any chance that vegetation interrupts your camera focusing on your primary subject, the bird's head *(35 mm SLR, 600 mm lens, 1/125 f 5.6, Kodachrome ISO 64)*. **Above, left:** Rosellas bathing, one such behaviour you can photograph when following this species *(35 mm SLR, 80–400 mm zoom lens, 1/125 f 5.6, Kodachrome ISO 64, handheld)*. **Above, right:** Composition and surrounds are as important to watch for as the main subject. One can at times (especially when a bird is relatively common and easy to approach), take less care of compositions *(35 mm SLR, 80–400 mm zoom lens, 1/125 f 5.6, Kodachrome ISO 64, handheld)*.

Birds on the Wing

What photographer does not love the idea of freezing a flying bird mid-air! Even the commonest of birds take on a whole new appeal when in flight. If this is an area of particular interest, you will love the technologies that are now developed to ensure this activity takes more than just luck. The new top of the range cameras provide a veritable array of aids. First and foremost is the ability of the camera to process large raw files driven by at least nine frames a second. Secondly, stunning multi-pattern metering systems and, finally, adjustable focusing systems enable you to program to suit your needs. Added to all this are high ISO ranges that produce virtually no noise. Then there are lenses with high speed servo focusing and if that's not enough, there is vibration reduction as well. All that is left to do is practice, which is easy enough to do at the beach working with sea gulls. However, these top of the range cameras and lenses are not cheap (little change out of ten thousand dollars) but this does not mean a less expensive version will not yield good results. Even high quality "point-and-shoot" compact cameras can do the job. Action photography, especially birds in-flight, is largely about practice.

Below: This Red-tailed Tropic Bird was photographed on Lady Elliott Island, Great Barrier Reef. During nesting, male and female birds care for the chick, and their mode of flight is usually easily tracked. Here, you can see the wonderful lighting on the wings. This is an effect caused by backlighting — that is the sun is behind and to the left of the bird *(35 mm SLR, 80–400 mm zoom lens, 1/500 f 5.6, Velvia ISO 100)*.

📷 QUICK TIP

- Sea birds and birds-of-prey are the two easiest groups of birds to photograph on the wing. In fact, practicing on sea gulls is a great way to perfect your skills. However, you will find even great in-flight shots of sea gulls are a challenge.

- Zoom lenses are very handy when photographing birds in-flight — start wide and then slowly zoom in.

- Another tip is to use a 35 mm SLR camera and auto focus lenses. However, the quality of the auto focus will vary.

Top: Birds flying directly towards you can be a focus problem. However, by using the camera's continuous auto focus the task is simplified *(35 mm DSLR, 80–400 mm zoom lens, 1/500 f5.6, ISO 320 RAW)*. **Above:** Because Pelicans are large and slow moving, head-on flight shots are relatively easy *(35 mm DSLR, 80–400 mm zoom lens, 1/500 f5.6, ISO 320 RAW)*. **Right:** A side on view is a simple matter of tracking the bird and making a series of photographs *(35 mm DSLR, 80–400 mm zoom lens, 1/500 f5.6, ISO 320 RAW)*.

Spiders & Insects

Photographing spiders and insects is a rewarding pastime. They are such small, often insignificant creatures to most people. However, a close-up photograph showing detail and colour can change that attitude. There are four basic ways to work them. The first is to drop to the ground almost anywhere and take a very close look. This can be a good thing to do awaiting sunset in front of a luscious landscape setting. The second is to pick a picturesque setting and attract them with water, flowers, minerals or decaying matter. This can be a quick way to get you close to potential subjects. The third way is to set-up your camera and go hunting (remembering, a little study goes a long way in tracking down various species). The fourth technique is to collect the animals and bring them home to photograph in a staged set-up. This is particularly good for photographing life cycles of butterflies and moths. My aim is to photograph animals as I encounter them in their world, paying special attention to those with interesting behavioural or visual appeal, although I have used the alternatives.

📷 QUICK TIP

- Both compact and 35 mm SLR cameras are fine for invertebrate photographing, although if you wish to perform selective focus and manage your backgrounds with some care, you will find the SLR a lot easier.

- Being such small animals, you will need to photograph with a macro lens, preferably 105 mm or a zoom micro lens. For very small insects you may need to add close-up lens attachments or extension tubes.

- For flash, I use a twin-flash (see page 12) and where possible add a third flash for backlighting. Flashes can be used as a total source of light (particularly when working with nocturnal insects) or alternatively, as a fill-in flash to reduce shadows. The more sophisticated flash units can be adjusted so that the flash output can be controlled, even when set on automatic. For instance, if your primary light source is neutral and you simply wish to fill-in shadows, or throw a little colour in, then you can adjust your flash to throw light that may be only one or two f-stops under the ambient light.

- Insects may be encountered day or night. An abundance of species can be found especially around lamps at night.

- Management of depth of field and selective focus is the same close-up as through any lens. However, the focus with extreme close-ups may be even more critical and understanding the relationship between apertures and shutter speeds, and how depth of field can be managed, is really essential.

- Watch your backgrounds. Aesthetic backgrounds will enhance your spider and insect photos.

- Invertebrates can be habitat-specific, so be careful about moving them from one plant to another. If you wish to move them, perhaps to photograph life cycles of moths and butterflies, you will need to be aware of their food plants.

Above: There are many ways to approach a subject as seen by the images on this page. You may choose the eye of a scientist, demanding perfect detail, or perhaps through the eye of an artist wishing to interpret more elements that evoke emotion. Spiders and insects offer a wonderful opportunity to work in both worlds.

Early morning or late afternoon is the best time to photograph butterflies. This is when they are basking in the sun and are more likely to remain still. If mating, they can be particularly sensitive and it is best to follow them until they are actually copulating. Moths, being primarily nocturnal, are best photographed at night — unless you find them hiding in the shadows roosting during the day. Moths do exhibit a strong eye-shine so finding them in the dark is comparatively easy if you use a head torch.

With butterflies, try to increase the working distance by using a long focal length lens such as 150 mm or 200 mm. This reduces the risk of casting a shadow across the animal. If your lens is not a close focus macro telephoto lens, try using either extension tubes or a close-up lens attachment. Overall, moths and butterflies offer endless challenges and are an interesting group of animals to photograph.

Clockwise from top left: Joseph's Coat Moth is one of the more spectacular Australian moths, making a great sequential subject from caterpillar, through cocoon building, then finally into a stunning adult *(all photographs with 35 mm DSLR, 70–180 mm micro zoom, 1/60 f 32, lens, ISO 320 RAW, twin macro flash units)*.

📷 QUICK TIP

- Insects are sensitive to temperature and bask in the sun to warm their flight muscles. Be careful not to breathe directly on the insects as you can increase the insect's temperature enough to cause them to take flight.

- When you are within 3 m of your quarry, move slowly. This is because most insects have compound eyes, which are very sensitive to movement.

- Avoid casting your shadow over the subject as this will either cause them to rearrange their position to find the light or to take flight.

Top: If using a net to capture butterflies for photography, it is important to use one with a soft netting so not to damage the animals. When you remove the butterfly take care when handling it. **Above:** A compact camera may be an advantage when approaching butterflies.

Above: This Evening Brown had settled in a darkened area. Using a tripod and a slow shutter speed that corresponded with the light output of my flash, I was able to balance the background and make the picture appear more natural *(35 mm DSLR, 70–180 mm micro zoom lens, 1/15 f16, ISO 320 RAW, twin macro flashes and tripod).* **Below:** Due to heavy rain and flowering plants, the population of Blue Tiger Butterflies exploded in the bush near my home *(35 mm DSLR, 70–180 mm micro zoom lens, 1/125 f16, ISO 320 RAW, twin macro flashes).*

Beetles, Bugs & more Insects

What is the difference between a bug and a beetle? The answer is in the mouthparts. Beetles have strong "jaws" for biting and chewing their prey, while bugs have a sharp, straw-like tube they use to pierce their food and suck its juices. Bugs usually have two pairs of wings. Beetles also have two pairs of wings but the forewings have been hardened into a protective covering. Apart from moths and butterflies, there are 23 large orders of invertebrate animals that we refer to commonly as beetles and bugs. This is a wonderful group of animals to concentrate your photography towards. It represents a very large number of species with a wonderfully diverse range of size, form and colour. Their behaviour can also be very different. My own experience has shown that peoples' attitudes towards bugs change when they see intimate close-up photographs of the animals.

Above: This photograph of a dragonfly was taken with the lens moved down to ensure the whole insect, including the lilly leaf and water drops, were in focus *(35 mm SLR, 200 mm micro lens, 1/125 f 22, Kodachrome ISO 64)*. **Left:** This dragonfly was taken with the lens deliberately wide open so that I could get the shortest depth of field possible. The white refractions at the top of the picture are out of focus highlights *(35 mm SLR, 200 mm micro lens, 1/250 f 5.6, Kodachrome ISO 64)*.

📷 QUICK TIP

- Generally speaking, getting close to beetles and bugs is relatively easy. Although, dragonflies can be as sensitive as butterflies and often require longer focal length close-up lenses. Nonetheless, I still prefer to use a longer focal length close-up lens on "the bugs".

- Beetles and bugs are active both day and night, although day shots with lighter coloured backgrounds can be more visually appealing.

Top, left: A large breeding female stick insect photographed with flash fill-in against a bright overcast sky. You can see the nice vibrant leaves. This is a result of the sun being directly behind the leaves *(35 mm DSLR, 70–180 mm micro zoom lens, 1/125 f 16, ISO 200 RAW, twin macro flashes)*. **Above:** Photographed in daylight in deep shade (hence the dark background), this Assassin Bug was feeding on a beetle and moving around a lot so I used a slow shutter speed on a tripod *(35 mm DSLR, 70–180 mm micro zoom lens, 1/60 f 32, ISO 320 RAW, twin macro flashes)*. **Centre, left:** These Fiddler Beetles have been photographed mating. This is just one of many activities that you can record *(35 mm DSLR, 70–180 mm micro zoom lens, 1/60 f 32, ISO 320 RAW, twin macro flashes)*. **Bottom, left:** Sometimes a portrait of an insect, like these Cicadas, can make very dramatic pictures. If your lens does not let you get this close, you could try a close-up attachment (like a filter) that you can attach to the front of your existing lens *(35 mm DSLR, 70–180 mm micro zoom lens, 1/60 f 32, ISO 320 RAW, twin macro flashes)*.

Spiders

Primitive spiders live underground in moist tunnels that enable them to breathe through their gill-like lungs called "book lungs". Because their eyesight is not very good, they sit just at the entrance to their burrow and wait patiently for an insect to come close enough for them to see. When they do see prey, they burst from the burrow and pounce on it with amazing speed. The burrows of these spiders are lined with silk from their abdomens, but they don't use the silk to spin a web. They sometimes nest in between cracks in rocks, logs, and tree-trunks. The hunters, jumpers and weavers, unlike primitive spiders, are a modern group of spiders that have excellent eyesight. They can live well away from a burrow and have invented some very interesting ways of catching their prey. Some hunt and pounce on their prey while others set "invisible" traps and some build beautiful strong, sticky webs. Modern spiders come in all shapes, sizes and colours. When they bite, their fangs work like a pair of tweezers to grip and move their prey around. The squeezing force can be so strong that it can sometimes even crush an insect's body! Welcome to the very popular world of spider photography — a challenging and fascinating group of animals to work with indeed.

Above: The Tent Spider builds a large tent-shaped web. Then, like other web hunters, sits back and simply waits for prey, which in this case is a fat cicada *(35 mm DSLR, 70–180 mm micro zoom lens, 1/60 f 22, ISO 320 RAW, twin micro flash)*.

Above: This Garden Orb-weaver is weaving a web at night. To highlight the threads of the web position I used one flash on top of the camera and held another behind to backlight the web. This same technique can be used during the day by positioning yourself down and letting natural light backlight the web while you fill-in the shadow with your flash *(35 mm DSLR, 70–180 mm micro zoom lens, 1/125 f 22, ISO 320 RAW, twin micro flash)*.

📷 QUICK TIP

- When flash is used with spiders on a solid substrate, you need to be aware of the shadow cast from your flash (eight shadows in fact). If you are using a twin flash system, then it is a good idea to adjust one flash so that it is about a half an f-stop less powerful than the other. This then acts as a fill-in of the shadows created by the other flash. Alternatively, a ring-flash or even better still natural light can be used.

Top: This Jewelled Spider was very small and the wind was playing havoc with my focus. Fortunately, the spider was rigging its web, so I waited until it came back to a branch to attach its web and then photographed it *(35 mm DSLR, 70–180 mm micro zoom lens, 1/60 f 16, ISO 320 RAW, twin micro flashes)*. **Above, left to right:** This large Huntsman Spider was photographed deep inside a cave while I was photographing microbats. It belongs to a common family of large spiders that frequent houses. In fact, I have large residents in most rooms of my house *(35 mm DSLR, 70–180 mm micro zoom lens, 1/60 f 16, ISO 320 RAW, twin micro flashes)*; The Flower or Crab Spider is an ambush hunter. When on flowering vegetation it will hide beneath petals and leaves pouncing on and stinging unwary visitors *(35 mm DSLR, 70–180 mm micro zoom lens, 1/125 f 16, ISO 320 RAW, twin micro flashes)*; Jumping spiders belong to the largest family of spiders in the world and are commonly encountered. Like many species, they are a lurking predator and some species can jump long distances. **Right:** This picture shows how a jumping spider behaves when threatened, stretching and flattening its body down a small stick. As you move, so does the spider so that it remains on the opposite side to the threat — a bit tricky to photograph *(35 mm DSLR, 70–180 mm micro zoom lens, 1/125 f 16, ISO 320 RAW, twin micro flashes)*.

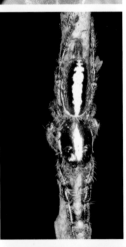

Dangerous to Man

There are several species of spider that can give a lethal bite. So, if you are working with spiders it does pay to do your research!

Marine Fish & Sea Mammals

In the recent past, the number of people making pictures of these animals in their natural habitat could be counted on one hand. Today, it is another matter altogether. Marine vertebrates are an extremely popular area for photographers. I believe this is due to the growth in dive schools, charters, importing of excellent, safe, reasonably priced dive gear, and the array of underwater photographic equipment now available. This also applies to the photography of invertebrates.

What has gladdened my heart over the 40 years I have watched underwater photography expand as a pastime, is the number of marine biologists that have taken to the sea with cameras. When I first started, the marine scientists that specialised in marine vertebrates didn't even go snorkelling! In fairness, not many people did in the 1950s. Today, many amateur naturalists and professional marine scientists document, study and share their knowledge of these stunning creatures. We need the pictures and we need this knowledge if we are to protect animals, which, for the most part, go unseen by the great majority of people. Let's face it — it is hard to inspire environmental concern, when most have never personally experienced the habitat of these amazing animals. Many people may never go underwater, but they can engage via photographs.

Above: Photographing the wonderful world of marine vertebrates is a rewarding pastime.

📷 QUICK TIP

- A basic underwater photographic kit — flash, or two, a housing and a digital camera — can range in price from a few thousand dollars to fifteen thousand. Interestingly, even the lower end cameras can make wonderful pictures. For beginners, turn to page 111 for my suggested websites and start with the less expensive brands, until you are sure you want to stick with it.

- One way to determine what brand of housing camera to go with is to look at the work of some of the experienced underwater photographers and see what they are using. My current kit is a 15 mm rangefinder Nikonos (no longer in manufacture) and a Nikonos RS underwater kit with twin sea strobes. Both rigs are film based, and parts are not readily available so I will be changing to digital sometime in the future.

Seals, Sea-lions, Whales & Dolphins

You would need a heart of steel not to be moved emotionally by this group of animals. However, capturing that feeling so that others can share it is another matter altogether. Apart from seals and sea-lions basking on the beach or rocks, marine mammals are an inherently difficult group to photograph well. In the world of professional wildlife photography, those that do best in this field do specialise and generally work outside Australian waters. Primarily due to a combination of water clarity (Australian conditions are not as good as other areas) and also the government restrictions on approaching whales. Nonetheless, while seals and sea-lions can be approached underwater, as can dolphins, whales can be photographed from licensed whalewatching boats in all Australian States.

Left: An Australian Fur-seal pup frolics in front of my camera in the shallow clear waters of Bass Strait. Pups can be extremely curious but take care with big bulls during the mating season *(35 mm rangefinder, 15 mm lens, 1/125 f 11, Velvia ISO 100)*.
Above: Sunning after a long swim in a cold ocean, this female Australian Sea-lion has returned to the beach to feed her young pup. Unlike other marine mammals, the seals and sea-lions have a terrestrial story to photograph *(35 mm, SLR, 80–400 mm zoom lens, 1/125 f 16, Velvia ISO 100)*.

Under the Whale Protection Act 1980, persons must avoid all contact with whales and calves. There is also State-specific legislation in place. For example, the Qld Nature Conservation Act 1992, guidelines state boats must be no closer than 100 m to a whale, and a person must not enter the water closer than 300 m to a whale.

Right, top to bottom: The arching backs of Humpback Whales during their migration north to breed. This is the sort of picture you are more likely to get on a whalewatching tour *(35 mm SLR, 80–400 mm zoom lens, 1/125 f16, Velvia ISO 100, handheld)*; After a day of photographing the backs of passing whales, I was lucky to make a nice sequence of images of two young males frolicking. The activity lasted five minutes. So, persistence is essential when photographing on whale tours; don't expect stunning images on your first day. You might have to keep trying *(35 mm SLR, 600 mm lens, 1/125 f5.6, Velvia ISO 100)*; Along Australia's southern coast you are likely to see and, if you are fortunate, photograph two species — the Humpback Whale and the Southern Right Whale. This photograph was taken on the south-west coast of WA. The females spend some months lolling in the clear, shallow waters feeding and caring for their young. This photograph was taken from a light aircraft *(35 mm SLR, 80–400 mm zoom lens, 1/500 f8, Velvia ISO 100, handheld)*; Swimming with and photographing dolphins in the wild is possible in a few places in most Australian States and these animals can provide a thrilling photographic experience *(35 mm SLR, 80–400 mm zoom lens, 1/500 f8, Velvia ISO 100, tripod)*.

📷 QUICK TIP

- Natural light and multi-pattern metering using an ISO around 400 on your digital camera is the best way to set-up for underwater photographs of marine mammals. I would suggest that you adjust contrast, hue and colour temperature during your post-production.

- Either extreme wide-angle lenses, or preset shutter speed and aperture will be essential as you will have little time for making adjustments.

The small bottom-dwelling carpet sharks, cat sharks, wobbegongs, Port Jackson Shark and their close allies represent the majority of shark species encountered by photographers. Members of the whaler family mainly represent the larger reef sharks seen during a dive. Although, if you are very lucky you may see a Whale Shark, or a Hammerhead, Tiger or Mako Shark, usually passing by in the distant haze. Whatever the encounter, sharks are a highlight for photographers. Photographers largely ignore the rays, apart from the Mantas, probably due to their lack of colour and general visual appeal. As a result of this "lack of appeal", the rays have not been at the forefront of the broader communities consciousness when it comes to understanding the role they play in a reef ecosystem. We photographers need to change that.

Above: Without doubt the Manta Ray is one of the most exciting vertebrate animals you will ever encounter. They move slowly, so there is usually time to set-up a shot before they vanish into the blue *(35 mm rangefinder, 15 mm lens, 1/125 f 5.6, Kodachrome ISO 64).*

Sharks are designed to merge into their background, and escape early detection by their prey. This allows them to get close enough to make a strike. The photograph of a whaler (opposite) is a classic example of the "merging" I refer to. In some instances, these sorts of pictures reproduce so poorly that we are forced to make digital computer adjustments to increase contrast. It is also possible to use electronic flash to overcome this problem and if you are lucky enough to be able to photograph close to the surface, the colour contrast could be considerably better. Contrast can also be improved if the animal is passing over a lighter coloured sandy sea floor (opposite).

📷 QUICK TIP

- Generally speaking, even if photographing ground sharks and bottom-dwelling rays and their relatives, it is best to use wide-angle lenses and high ISO ratings to enable a depth of field that reveals the entire animal in focus.

- If unable to shoot midwater rays and sharks close to the surface or light-coloured sea floor, make adjustments to your RAW digital files to increase contrast. It is also possible to use electronic flash to overcome this issue, and if lucky enough to photograph close to the surface, the colour contrast could be considerably better.

Above: Most stingrays rest on the sea floor when not feeding. In fact, when inactive, they generally cover themselves with sand *(6 x 6 SLR, 50 mm lens, 1/125 f 16, Ektacrome ISO 64, electronic flash).*

Top: Sharks tend to merge with the background *(35 mm rangefinder, 15 mm lens, 1/125 f 8, Velvia ISO 100).* **Above:** Note the contrast between the shark's colour tones and the sandy substrate beyond *(35 mm rangefinder, 15 mm lens, 1/60 f 16, Velvia ISO 100, flash fill-in).*

Danger to Photographers

The great majority of rays and sharks are harmless and those recorded as dangerous to man — sharks in particular — are restricted to a very small number of species. Animals like the White Shark, Bull Shark, Tiger Shark, Mako Shark and a number of smaller whalers, have either bitten or, in a small number of cases, killed humans. However, in most cases, the attacks have been on swimmers, spear fishers, fishers and divers provoking the animals either deliberately or unintentionally. Divers with considerable shark experience believe the chance of an attack on a SCUBA diver making pictures on the sea floor (particularly a diver not behaving aggressively) would be extremely unlikely. If you are new to underwater photography and have concerns, it is best to research the areas that you plan to dive and to question your local marine parks or fisheries department and obtain on-site advice before entering the water.

A stingray will not bite you. However, it may, if handled or threatened in any way, raise the barb on its tail, lunge up with its body, and stab what it considers to be a threat to its safety. Not all rays have poisonous barbs. There are two records of stingrays causing death. Stingrays are by nature shy animals and in most instances the majority of species will swim away as you approach.

Pelagic Fish

While there are many challenges in getting close to pelagic (or open water) fish, schooling fish can be more daunting. They occupy open water where predators are swift, so they swim in schools for defence. When you are stalking them, it's not one fish you have to contend with, but hundreds. Spook one, and they are all gone.

Another challenge is to obtain evenly illuminated and well-exposed shots. Integral to their defence are their shiny, reflective scales, which reflect the colours of the surrounding water. So, if you illuminate them side on for photography you are likely to finish up with a series of unappealing "hot spots" in the picture. Lighting the fish on an angle can overcome this problem.

📷 QUICK TIP

- Pelagic fish form large usually tightly packed schools, especially when under threat. If you are descending or ascending, or hanging off the anchor line decompressing, schools may approach closely. Generally speaking, a school of fish is difficult to pursue, as they are capable of considerable speed.

- The best angle for making a photograph of schooling fish is towards the surface from slightly below. This helps both with flash reflection and also gives a lighter, brighter background.

Opposite: Trevallies are one of the largest families of pelagic fish in Australia *(35 mm SLR, 20–36 mm zoom lens, 1/1000 f 5.6, Kodachrome ISO 64).* **Top:** Schooling fish in silhouette can make dramatic pictures. Particularly, if you are fortunate enough to have open water predators milling around the outer parameters of the swirling central mass *(35 mm SLR, 15 mm lens, 1/125 f 5.6, Velvia ISO 100).*

Above: Pelagic species are sometimes seen alone, although it is likely that the main school is close by. This large solitary kingfish is probably patrolling the shallows *(35 mm SLR, 20–36 mm zoom lens, 1/60 f 8, Kodachrome ISO 64, electronic flash).*

Sedentary & Marauding Predatory Fish

Known as sedentary and marauding predators, this group falls into two categories. Firstly, there are fish that are sedentary in their behaviour and spend the majority of their time sitting on the sea floor. These fish are usually very cryptic in colour and pattern (like soles, flatheads, hawkfish, some species of scorpionfish etc). The second category, includes the marauding carnivores like lionfish and rockcod that usually move slowly around the reef, increasing speed only when striking at prey. From a photographic perspective, these fish are some of the more spectacular species to shoot and are so convinced of their own camouflage they are much easier for photographers to approach.

Above: The Longnose Hawkfish like all the hawkfish is, as its name implies, a fish with keen eyesight that rests on the corals and waits until it spots a small crustacean. Then, with alarming speed, it strikes *(35 mm SLR, 55 mm micro lens, 1/125 f 22, Velvia ISO 100)*. **Opposite, top:** Lionfish are an excellent example of the slow-moving marauding carnivores. They are also a group of fish that underwater photographers love to photograph due to their dramatic trailing fins. And they are one of the easiest groups of fish to approach *(35 mm SLR, 20–36 mm zoom lens, 1/60 f 16, Velvia ISO 100, electronic flash)*. **Opposite, left:** Photographers are always ready to look into the caves, fissures and under ledges for sedentary and marauding predators. Especially those species that spend daylight hours hidden, waiting for either twilight or total darkness to feed. These are the soldier, rockcod, sea perch, knight, and cardinalfish, among many other species *(35 mm SLR, 20–36 mm zoom lens, 1/60 f 16, Velvia ISO 100, electronic flash)*. **Opposite, right:** Well known to underwater photographers, the Red Rockcod has quite remarkable camouflage. It is only when using an electronic flash that its true colours are revealed *(6 x 6 SLR, 80 mm lens extension tubes, 1/125 f 22, Ektachrome ISO 64, electronic flash)*.

📷 QUICK TIP

- As you make your final adjustments to focus, it is worthwhile holding your breath so that the masterpiece you are about to create is not spoilt by bubble eruptions that frighten your quarry.

- In regard to lenses and lighting set-ups, refer to the information on roving reef fish on the following pages.

Mobile Reef Fish

Of all the groups of animals represented in this book, none gives me more personal pleasure to photograph than these spectacular animals. Mobile reef fish spend their days avoiding predators and feeding or searching for partners to mate with. When I first began photographing fish back in the 1960s, not much was known about fish behaviour. In fact, many species were not even scientifically classified. Nowadays, most have been described and there are some excellent books that help identify them. As far as documented information of their behaviour is concerned, there is far less known. This is mainly because professional fish scientists work primarily with fish that have a commercial interest. Nonetheless, web research will find some species' behaviour described. This will give you at least a head start in identifying those many curious activities that you will be photographing. As far as getting close enough to make frame filling pictures, mobile fish do fall into certain categories — four primary are discussed here.

Above: This leatherjacket represents those species that are more likely to "prop" in front of the camera, even if only briefly. The problem with pursuing fish is that you can stir up the bottom debris, spoiling the clear images needed *(6x6 SLR, 50 mm lens, f125 f16, Ektachrome ISO 64, single flash, 15 metres)*.

📷 QUICK TIP

- In the 35 mm format, I would suggest either 35 mm, 55 mm micro or 105 mm micro lenses for mobile reef fish. Large species or schooling species require a wider lens. I use a 55 mm micro and a 20 to 36 mm zoom lens. When you have gathered most species in your area with these lenses you might try a 105 mm lens for those smaller fish or ones you couldn't get close to.

Above, left: Cleaning stations can be great places to make close-ups, simply because the act of parasite-removal activity occupies the fish *(35 mm SLR, 50 mm lens, f125 f16, Ektachrome ISO 64, single flash)*. **Above, right:** One of the more artful challenges with photographing constantly mobile fish is to make pictures that are composed of the fish in its surrounding habitat. Fish, like this female Crimson Wrasse, will often come to investigate — but only briefly so respond quickly. As soon as the fish loses interest in you, it will be a big task for you to hunt down that individual again *(6x6 SLR, 50 mm lens, f125 f16, Ektachrome ISO 64, single flash, 15 metres)*.

Mobile Fish at Night

Returning to your favourite dive site at night, you may find many of the familiar fish that lurk in the dark caves and crevices and under ledges during the day are out and about feeding. Of the more familiar daylight-active fish, many wedge into crevices fast asleep and many change their colours from the normal bright hues to drab and mottled colours. You might even see species you have never seen before. Dive with a buddy and carry a powerful lantern, preferably attached to your camera, for focus.

Below: Both bannerfish (below, right) and parrotfish (below, left) are sleeping and have adjusted their colours and body markings *(both photographs: 6x6 SLR, 50 mm lens, f125 f16, Ektachrome ISO 64, single flash)*.

Marine Invertebrates

Comprising the majority of animal species on Earth, invertebrates (soft-bodied animals with no cartilaginous or bony structure) are found in multitudes beneath the sea. And, when it comes to form, texture, shape and most certainly colour, they are the most photogenic of all animals groups. They also represent the least known animals on Earth and this is where the challenge lies for photographers.

In the late 1960s, it was fish that took my fancy, and for some years I just could not see beyond my newfound, all-absorbing hobby. However, I soon discovered that most fish relied on the invertebrates for survival. Whether for food or for shelter, I learned that many had fascinating symbiotic relationships — the anemonefish and the anemone are examples. So, without even making a conscious decision, I found myself an avid collector of marine invertebrate photographs. This is a very addictive world, so beware!

Clockwise from top left to centre: Anemone; Ascidians; Sea star; Urchin; Slipper coral; Sea pen; Gorgonian coral; Feather star; Sea star. It is hard not to look at marine invertebrates, particularly close-up, and not see a piece of art.

📷 QUICK TIP

- Most 35 mm DSLR cameras can be put in tailor-made underwater housing. You will find a plethora of options on the internet. You will also find all the accessories, like strobes (electronic flashes), flash arms and ports for the various focal length lenses. Beginners can start with a kit that comes with the camera and all accessories needed to get started.

- Much like fish, to photograph the world of invertebrates either a zoom lens, or a fixed focal length lens is required. This will allow you to photograph a reef scene, and make a close-up focus on smaller individual animals, like sea stars. Also consider the need for two electronic flash units which should create nice shadowless lighting when working up close. You can consider that marine invertebrate photography is much like photographing insects and spiders on land — the same principals apply.

- Exploring the world of invertebrates, you will be tempted to move the mobile invertebrates into more photogenic settings. However, do not place them on substrates that they would not normally inhabit. For example, a sea star found on the sand, may inhabit that world permanently, so moving it on top of a piece of coral would mean it was in an unnatural habitat.

Motile & Sessile Invertebrates

MOTILE INVERTEBRATES

The molluscs (shells, octopus, squid), the echinoderms (sea stars, feather stars, brittle stars, basket stars, urchins and sea cucumbers), crustaceans (crabs, crays, prawns and shrimps) and the annelids (the worms) are the main groups of motile invertebrates. Some, like the cephalopods (octopus, squid and cuttles), are considered to be the most mobile and intelligent of all invertebrates, including land-based species. This is a fascinating world filled with excitement for underwater photographers.

Below: Coral and rock reefs can feature a sea floor entirely covered with a variety of sessile invertebrate animals. In the cracks and crevices, the motile invertebrates are found. Up to 20 or 30 of each group can cover an area of two square metres *(35 mm SLR, 50 mm lens, f 125 f 16, Ektachrome ISO 64, single flash)*.

SESSILE INVERTEBRATES

Most cnidarians (corals, anemones, hydroids and tube anemones), poriferans (sponges), bryozoans (moss animals, sometimes called lace corals, although they are not corals), ascidians (sea squirts), and even some worms and crustaceans, spend their entire lives attached to the sea floor or some other surface, sessile. A quality lantern attached to the camera housing is extremely handy, not just for night diving but also for focusing in darkened areas. Many interesting species live beneath ledges and deep inside caves and crevices. I suggest to overweight yourself slightly so that you can kneel or lie on the bottom without moving. This will reduce sediment disturbance and assist in concentration for the tasks of focusing and composing.

Top: An electronic flash will be required to bring out the colour and detail of all invertebrates, like this delicate worm. The living colours of these animals can be surprising *(6x6 SLR, 80 mm with extension tubes, 1/125 f22, Ektachrome ISO 64, electronic flash)*. **Above, left:** This Common Octopus is flushing grey, a colour believed to be a sign of fear. The octopus, and its relative the cuttlefish, are two molluscs that are interesting to photograph, due to their animated behaviour *(6x6 SLR, 50 mm, 1/125 f22, Ektachrome ISO 64, electronic flash)*. **Above, centre:** These sea whip anemones were photographed in deep temperate water, so dark in fact, a torch was needed to focus *(6x6 SLR, 80 mm with extension tube, 1/125 f22, Ektachrome ISO 64, electronic flash)*. **Above, right:** These delicate and colourful shrimps are quite easy to approach with a close-up camera *(6x6 SLR, 80 mm with extension tube, 1/125 f22, Ektachrome ISO 64, electronic flash)*.

📷 QUICK TIP

- While automatic focus is an option underwater, I prefer to fix my focus, adjust my electronic flashes to suit the area needing illumination, then rock the camera back and forth until focus is sharp. This only applies to an SLR camera with a viewing port.

- For extreme macro photographs, much like insects on land, a 55 mm, 105 mm, and a 200 mm micro lens is best. For wider-angle shots of a reef scene, or a large mobile invertebrate like an octopus, try a 35 mm or even 20 mm lens.

Aquariums

The opportunities to make images in the freshwater field are restricted by a number of factors. Freshwater rivers, billabongs, lakes and wetlands are generally shallow, so it is hard to move around underwater without stirring up a cloud of mud and vegetation detritus, completely obliterating visibility. There are some localities featuring a combination of depth, crystal-clear water and even, rocky substrates allowing great photographs. However, getting close enough to the quarry can be very challenging. The freshwater photography enthusiast usually chooses to capture their quarry with nets and move them into freshwater aquariums to make pictures (permits may be required). While this sounds easy, it does require considerable patience, skill and knowledge because a wild-caught fish transferred to a small aquarium does not necessarily mean the animal is going to cooperate. The first thing they are likely to want to do is hide. Thus, be prepared to wait until the animal is settled and the water has cleared before taking photographs.

Left: An example of an enthusiast's freshwater aquarium that can be set up in one's home.

📷 QUICK TIP

- While compact cameras are popular these days, more and more keen photographers are moving to SLRs. The advantage of an SLR camera, when photographing into aquariums, is that you can manage the final outcome. Advantages, as discussed throughout this book, are particularly magnified when managing internal room reflections on the surface of the aquarium as you can easily see them. The fold-out screen on a compact camera needs to be held at a distance from the eye, so it is a lot easier to miss reflections. Reflections at home may come from a number of sources, such as open windows, TV screens, light-coloured objects in the room and so on. Even in commercial aquariums there may be reflection issues, although most have the outer areas dimly lit to combat this. The closer to the front of the glass the less reflections will be encountered. In some circumstances, I have even cupped my hands around the front of the lens to reduce light. A soft rubber lens hood could help in these situations also.

- For frame-filling pictures of small fish, a micro lens at around 105 mm to 200 mm is ideal. For wider shots of either the entire aquarium, or larger fish, try a 55 mm lens. I use a 70–180 mm micro zoom lens exclusively for all photographs in aquariums.

Clockwise from top: A rainbow fish; This rare Freshwater Sawfish was photographed using natural light; A large, healthy Murray Spiny Crayfish; A Murray Cod, an icon among freshwater fish *(all taken with 35 mm DSLR, 70–180 mm micro zoom lens, ISO 320 RAW, single top mounted electronic flash, photographs from freshwater aquariums around Australia).*

PHOTOGRAPHING IN AQUARIUMS

For excellent examples of clear, compelling images made in aquariums check out our *Wild Australia Guides* on *Freshwater Turtles* and *Freshwater Fishes*. This work, created by John Cann and Gunther Schmida respectively, is the result of years of careful, patient collecting, and studying the species' behaviour. Of course, there is also the willingness to put in the work required to manage their aquariums.

ELECTRONIC FLASH POSITIONING

By using a digital camera it is easy to discover if the positioning of the flash is incorrect, as white flares will be seen in the images. This is caused by the flash bouncing off the glass. If using a long micro lens (105 mm to 200 mm), it is possible to attach the flash to the top of the camera, although there will be a need to shoot on a slight angle and not directly on the glass front. This approach is good for public aquariums. At home, I mount two flash units on small tripods to the left and right of the camera angled at 45° at the front of the aquarium. Do tests of your set-up to see how far forward and backward to move the camera. And also test how much latitude for your flash coverage, remembering the fish swims up and down (left and right) in the aquarium.

FOCUS AND DEPTH OF FIELD

The principles that apply to photographing small animals up close, also apply to photographing animals in aquariums. Personally, I am a fan of soft, simple backgrounds. This helps define the form and shape of a fish when it is midwater. This, however, does not apply to animals on the bottom of the tank. Depending on the vegetation in the tank, and particularly how far behind the subject the vegetation is, soften the background by using a small f-stop number. Therefore, reducing the depth of field. If featuring the surrounding plants or rocks, then a wider area of field will be necessary (and thus, a larger f-stop number).

CLEAN, CLEAR GLASS

Photographing in any of Australia's public aquariums can be a problem, unless the glass is clean and flat. Many commercial aquariums use thick plastic walls, some are even curved. This can cause optical problems. Scratches on the glass are always an issue — however, if you use a moderately long lens (such as a 105 mm or even a 200 mm lens) exclusively in these situations the depth of field can be adjusted to eliminate small scratches on the front of the glass. Also be sure the subject is some distance back from the glass — a few centimetres at least. If the subject is too close the depth of field will capture the scratches. Small scratches can be removed post-shoot with computer imaging software. If building an aquarium specifically for photography, consider the optical quality of the glass you are using.

Top: Freshwater yabbies and crays are popular tank exhibits and make interesting subjects to photograph *(35 mm DSLR, 70–180 mm micro zoom lens, 1/60 f 22, ISO 320 RAW single top mounted flash, photographed in an aquarium).*   **Above:** In the wild, the colours of the Purple-spotted Gudgeon are quite dark and cryptic. In the aquarium, under flashlight they are very colourful. This is a male (lower) and female (above) *(35 mm DSLR, 70–180 mm micro zoom lens, 1/60 f 22, ISO 320 RAW single top mounted flash, photographed in an aquarium).*

After the Field Trip

The technology used to reproduce images for print has advanced in leaps and bounds in recent years. Laborious techniques of the past have been rapidly overtaken and nowadays, digital or film images can be prepared on a modest home computer system. The sophistication of the hardware and software available to the amateur today, is on par with high end professional equipment accessible only five years ago.

If you wish to go beyond having your film developed or digital images processed by a laboratory, it is necessary to acquire some knowledge of the post-photographic-exposure digital world (known as post-production). With the explosion in popularity of digital cameras, the internet has almost become a giant photo album. There is a plethora of photo sharing sites for you to upload your images to share with the world at large.

You can mix still images with video and produce your own DVD (Digital Versatile [or Video] Disc) for screening. Gone are the static images in slide shows of yesteryear, with modern software you can create dynamic effects, panning and zooming across your photos to recreate a journey or convey the mood. Sharing images aside, you can correct any faults in images, manipulate them in many ways, including making them look like paintings. The opportunities for creative expression are as limitless as your imagination.

If you are an advanced amateur photographer, wishing to market your work, then some knowledge of digital technologies is essential in this modern world of electronic communication.

PRINT RESOLUTION GUIDE

The table below is a rough guide to the final print size you can expect to achieve from a digital camera.

CAMERA RESOLUTION	PRINT SIZE					
	4x6"	5x7"	8x10"	11x14"	16x20"	20x30"
2 Megapixel	Photo Quality	Photo Quality	Very Good	Acceptable	Acceptable	Poor
3 Megapixel	Photo Quality	Photo Quality	Excellent	Good	Acceptable	Acceptable
4 Megapixel	Photo Quality	Photo Quality	Photo Quality	Very Good	Good	Acceptable
5 Megapixel	Photo Quality	Photo Quality	Photo Quality	Excellent	Very Good	Very Good
6 Megapixel	Photo Quality	Photo Quality	Photo Quality	Photo Quality	Excellent	Very Good
7 Megapixel	Photo Quality	Photo Quality	Photo Quality	Photo Quality	Excellent	Excellent
8 Megapixel	Photo Quality	Photo Quality	Photo Quality	Photo Quality	Photo Quality	Excellent
10 Megapixel +	Photo Quality	Photo Quality	Photo Quality	Photo Quality	Photo Quality	Photo Quality

FILE FORMATS

When working with photographs it is important to always maintain the highest quality, and that being said working with TIFF files is the best option for correction and reproduction.

Shooting in JPEG format is fine, and may be the only option you have. It is important to know though — when you open, modify, then save that image as a JPEG you are effectively throwing information away. This is due to the compression algorithms used in the JPEG format (these are lossy, meaning that information is lost). If you shoot in JPEG, best practice is to open and correct your image in your chosen photo editor and then save as a TIFF file. This ensures you will always have the best available image ready to use for any purpose. If you need to email or upload to a website, saving a copy as a JPEG will yield beautiful results. Most software will now have specific options for converting images to certain sizes for web or email output.

JPEG: A format that loses quality in compression when some information is lost and cannot be reclaimed. Perfect for email and the web. Small file size, good image quality.

TIFF: The best option for long term storage of images that you plan to correct. Large file size, excellent image quality with lossless compression.

RAW: Not all cameras will have this file format. This format is essentially the raw image data captured by the camera. Better results can be achieved shooting in RAW, but time post-shoot is needed to make your images look the best. Specialised software is also needed to read and convert the RAW file format. This is supplied with the camera. You would always save this file as a TIFF.

BACKUP YOUR IMAGES

One important aspect post-shoot is to backup your files. It is a horrible process if your hard drive should fail and you have to re-build the operating system, let alone if you have lost all of your digital photographs.

There are many solutions and various ways to do this, CD, DVD, online, etc. External hard disks are the easiest and cheapest (over time) solution. For under $250 you can now purchase a 500 gigabyte (GB) drive. This is large enough to store tens of thousands of images.

Backing up your images needs to become a habit. Every week or post-shoot, connect your backup drive and copy your entire pictures folder to it. Some external drives come with software that can automate this process. Disconnect the drive and place in a safe place. If something should happen to your computer, all that needs reinstalling is software, your irreplaceable photos are safe.

Once the image is on your computer screen there are many ways to alter it. In fact, digital manipulation is an art form in its own right. It is possible to manipulate colour, crop, soften, brighten, and create a multitude of effects.

In our publishing work, the editing is performed by either a designer or by the prepress (or film) house that produces high quality scans on a drum scanner and prepares the work for the printing press. Designers and prepress professionals are highly skilled in the operation and management of these processes.

If you have not developed skills with editing suites, with a little practice, it is achievable to prepare images for emailing, internet or digital print formats. I believe to appreciate every aspect of the publishing process, will result in the creation of higher quality images. There are product manuals and many courses of study to assist with this quest.

When a non-digital image is prepared for publication it must be scanned, and may require additional preparation —.particularly in terms of brightness, contrast and colour adjustment. What to correct can be a matter of opinion and is usually directed by a designer or an art director. Skilful management of this phase requires considerable experience and makes the difference between a top quality and ordinary publication.

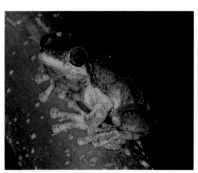 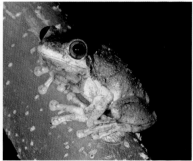

BRIGHTNESS AND CONTRAST

It is possible to lighten every pixel in the image or to lighten or darken sections of the image using the controls available in the editing software (above pictures).

COLOUR CORRECTION

Colours may be altered by controls or levels depending upon whether you want an overall effect or a single hue manipulated. Remember, variations in colour occur between monitors, printers, and film.

BLEMISHES

A sample colour or section may be duplicated from another part of the image then copied over an unwanted mark or object.

PHOTO-EDITING SOFTWARE

There are many photo-editing software applications available, from the simple to the sophisticated. Some computer packages include a selection of general applications, which may be useful (at least initially). It is a good place to start before investing in a full suite. Next, you might try shareware. Type "shareware photo-editing software" into a web search engine. It is surprising what is out there. Later, perhaps invest in a more specialised editing package to experiment and create exciting images.

Aperture and Lightroom, available from Apple and Adobe respectively, are sophisticated digital image management tools featuring many useful functions. These applications not only catalogue and colour correct your digital or scanned photos, but have many other practical tools for sharing your photos with others.

CROPPING

Cropping is used to fit an image into a particular area, or to change the emphasis of the original image. Some photographs lack good composition in the first place and may be dramatically enhanced through skillful cropping. This aspect of manipulation is something that can be creatively stimulating and, with practice,

may influence your approach to composition in the field. Cropping is used extensively in the production of photographic spreads when images must fit together to illustrate one or more predetermined concepts.

The most effective way to share images quickly with friends is by email. When attaching a small JPEG file to an email, you are sending a glimpse of your life. Events, people, special moments may range from the trivial to the momentous. To share images more widely and efficiently, create a website to display the best selection.

The simplest site is one featuring internet space and templates for text and images provided by the host. They are often free, but part of the deal could be advertising on your web page.

AN ONLINE PHOTO-IMAGE GALLERY

Look at various online galleries for ideas. They often show thumbnails (small versions) of their best images, at low resolution which you can click on to enlarge for a proper look. If someone downloaded your image, the resolution would not be sufficient to allow them to print it, which gives some copyright protection against theft of images. Write a note on your site for interested people to contact you if they wish to buy an image.

From within your photo gallery it is possible to provide:

- Screensavers and screen images created from images downloaded from your site are great, as long as the file size you have prepared is adequate for the screen enlargement.

- Clip art of small — usually less than 50 kb — picture files, often etches, that can be easily downloaded.

- A video clip can be prepared from digital video so that a viewer can watch a small presentation. This does require viewers to have good modem connection-speed.

- eGreetings require HTML coding skills. If you do not have the necessary coding skills, it is possible to provide a HTML tag on your site that will allow a third party to manage eGreetings for you.

- The opportunities to display images on a website are boundless and browsing through some of the many interesting sites will give you lots of ideas. Try typing "photo gallery" into your search engine.

Putting on a Show

There are many ways to share the excitement of your wildlife photographic adventures. High resolution TV screens, mobile phones, digital projections onto giant theatre screens, or giant wall prints for your home or for public exhibition can all be utilised. Approach photographic, conservation or local community organisations and discuss how to work together, possibly in a fundraising or community-awareness synergy. Maybe there are several photographers that want to be involved in exhibiting their work, or members of a photography club or a group that shares a common interest in a photographic theme that you can foster. Try to gain support from one or a number of local businesses in hosting the event. Just be aware that this kind of activity has to be planned thoroughly and make yourself aware of any obligations or responsibilities you might be taking on. Any of these activities could give your presentation an edge:

- Ask local musicians to perform live to the projected images.

- If one of the exhibitors is a poet or writer, consider a short reading during the presentation.

- Incorporate a theme that may attract the attention of the media and, in turn, promote your show.

- Consider asking a local identity to be MC for the evening.

Glossary

ANGLE OF VIEW The extent of the view taken in by a lens, determined by the focal length of the lens.

APERTURE A metal diaphragm through which a controlled amount of light passes to expose the film.

BACKLIGHT Light that comes from behind the subject and towards the camera lens. The subject may stand out in silhouette.

BRACKETING The technique of taking a number of photographs of the same subject, in quick sequence, at progressive levels of exposure.

COMPACT CAMERA A small automated camera with a fixed lens and direct vision viewfinder.

COMPOSITION The arrangement of the elements, the subject and other objects, in a scene or photograph.

DEPTH OF FIELD The distance between the nearest and farthest objects that appear in acceptably sharp focus in a photograph.

DIFFUSE LIGHTING Lighting that is low or moderate in contrast.

EXPOSURE The quantity of light allowed to pass through to the film.

EXTENSION TUBE A metal or plastic tube inserted between the lens and the camera, making the lens-to-film distance greater.

FAST FILM Film with an emulsion that is very sensitive to light.

FILL-IN An extra light source, such as flash, used to soften shadows caused by a brighter main light, such as the sun.

FILTER Transparent material placed over a lens to alter the nature, colour or quality of the light passing through it.

FLASH An artificial light source (a flashbulb or electronic flash unit) which illuminates a subject being photographed.

FLASH MEMORY CARD A storage medium used by most digital cameras. It substitutes for the film in conventional photography.

FOCAL LENGTH The distance between the film plane and the optical centre of the lens when the lens is focused at infinity.

FOCUS Adjustment of the setting of the focal length to sharply define the selected area of the scene or subject.

FOCUS LOCK A lever, button or switch that locks either the lens or body focus, depending on the type of camera.

FORMAT The size of the image area on a roll or sheet of film.

F-STOP A number that indicates the size of the aperture, hence the amount of light allowed to pass through the lens to the film.

IMAGE RESOLUTION The number of dots per inch (dpi) or pixels per inch (ppi) displayed in the printed length in an image.

ISO (International Standards Organisation). The speed rating for photographic film, the number represents the film's sensitivity to light. A higher ISO number indicates the film is more sensitive and requires less light for a proper exposure.

LENS A single piece of transparent material with at least one curved surface used to change the convergence of light rays.

LENS PERSPECTIVE Provides linear perspective, or the sense of depth and distance, in a two-dimensional photograph.

LENS SPEED The widest aperture (smallest f-stop) in relation to focal length which a lens can be set. A fast lens transmits more light than a slow lens.

LINEAR PERSPECTIVE A geometrical system for showing the apparent positions and magnitudes of objects to give the illusion of space and distance on a flat surface.

LONG LENS See telephoto lens.

MACRO LENS A lens that has continuous focusing capacity from infinity to 1:2 and extreme life-size 1:1 close-ups.

MATRIX METERING Light coming from a subject passes through the lens into a multi-segment light meter, and the camera sets aperture and shutter speed for the optimal exposure.

MEDIUM FORMAT A film (and camera) format providing a larger and better image than 35 mm size, suitable for commercial reproduction. The most popular sizes are 6x6 cm, 6x4.5 cm and 6x7 cm.

MONOPOD A one-legged support used to hold the camera steady.

MOTOR DRIVE An electronic mechanism for advancing the film to the next frame and resetting the shutter. Popular for action-sequence photography.

MULTI-PATTERN METERING For metering accurate exposure across unevenly lit subjects by dividing a scene into a matrix of separate cells, each of which can be metered independently to accurately calculate exposure when highlights and shadows exist outside the centre of the frame.

OVER-EXPOSE To set exposure so that too much light reaches the film, resulting in a dense negative or a light, washed-out transparency.

PANORAMA A broad view across a continuous expanse of the horizon.

PERSPECTIVE The visual representation of the three dimensions of depth and distance in a two-dimensional photograph.

PIXEL A single picture element of a digital photo. In a digital image each pixel is assigned a location and colour value.

RANGEFINDER A viewfinder included on many cameras as an aid in composing and, in some cases, focusing. Can cause parallax distortion.

RAW A file format containing the uncorrected image data captured by the camera sensor.

REFLECTOR Any surface from which light can be reflected on to a subject, usually into areas of shadow.

RESOLUTION The fineness of detail recorded in a photographic image or print.

SATURATION The perception of colour according to whether it displays more or less hue and brightness.

SCANNER A scanner is a device that captures analogue data (e.g. an image) and converts it to digital data, for input into a computer to display, edit, store, or output.

SHUTTER SPEED The amount of time for which the shutter stays open to light, measured in fractions of a second.

SLOW LENS A lens with a small maximum aperture (e.g. f8). The lens lets in less light, necessitating longer exposure times in low light.

SLR (Single Lens Reflex). A camera of 35 mm or medium format, in which a system of mirrors and prisms allows the viewing of a scene through the same lens that takes the picture.

SPOT METER A narrow-angle exposure meter that takes reflected light readings from a small area of a subject, and that can be used from some distance away.

STANDARD LENS A lens produces an image roughly similar to the original scene as perceived by the human eye. It has a focal length approximately equal to the diagonal of the film format (e.g. 50 mm for a 35 mm camera). Also called a normal lens.

TELEPHOTO LENS A lens with a focal length much greater than the diagonal of the film format (or standard lens) which it is used, e.g. 300 mm on 35 mm format, where the standard is 50 mm. It shows an enlarged section with a narrower angle of view than does a standard lens. Depth of field decreases as focal length increases. Can isolate a subject from a distance. Also called a long lens.

TTL (Through-the-Lens) camera. A type of camera that allows TTL metering and focusing.

TWILIGHT The time just before sunrise or just after sunset when the sky is lit by the sun's light but the sun is not visible.

UV FILTER A clear, colourless filter that absorbs ultra-violet radiation.

VIEWPOINT The position (above, below, far or near) relative to a photographic subject, which a shot is made.

WIDE-ANGLE LENS A lens which has a shorter focal length and a wider angle of view than a standard lens. Focal length is less than the diagonal of the film frame. In 35 mm photography, lenses from 24 to 35 mm are generally thought of as wide-angles, and those under 24 mm as ultra-wide. Depth of field increases as focal length decreases. Also called a short lens.

ZOOM LENS A lens of continuously variable focal length. In effect, many lenses of different focal lengths in one unit (e.g. 80–200 mm). Also called a variable focus lens.

Index

Online & Further Reading

Visit our dedicated Photograph Australia website **www.photographaustralia.com.au** and join our forum. The site also features an interactive map and extensive photo tips covering every aspect of photographing in Australia. Meet other keen photographers and exchange ideas — you can even enter our Photo of the Week competition!

Browse the internet and view the work of Australia's leading wildlife photographers

BG Wildlife Photographer of the Year 2006 **www.amonline.net.au/exhibitions/ travel/ wildlife_2006.htm**

Peter Merritt, Wildlife Photographer **www.merrittimages.com**

Nature's Image Photography, Landscape and Wildlife Images of Australia. Beginner's Guide to Photography **www.naturesimage.com.au**

Photographic gallery photographer, Pavel German **www.australiannature.com**

ANZANG Nature and Landscape: The Third Collection, Photographer of the Year, Exposing Nature. A Guide to Wildlife Photography **www.publish.csiro.au/nid/18/pid/5692.htm**

Underwater and Nature Photography **www.seanature.southcom.com.au**

David Cook Wildlife Photography **www.davidcook.com.au**

Graeme Chapman, renowned ornithologist and wildlife photographer **www.grahamchapman .com.au**

Wildlife photography by Ray Drew **www.raydrew.net/intro**

Nature photography by Paul Benjafield **www.wildprint.com.au**

Esther Beaton photographs and writes about Australia **www.estherbeaton.com**

Scott Portelli, Wildlife Photographer **www.scottportelli.com**

Exposing Nature. A Guide to Wildlife Photography. This book should appeal both to the novice and the more advanced nature photographer, go to: **www.publish.csiro.au/pid/5206.htm**

RSPB Guide to Digital Wildlife Photography. This is a helpful and practical guide to all aspects of digital wildlife photography, accessibly written by and beautifully illustrated, go to: **www.allenandunwin.com**

DISCLAIMER:

Where brand names are mentioned in this book the reader should in no way consider it an endorsement of the product. Steve Parish Publishing does not endorse commercial products, processes, or services. The views and opinions of the author may not be used for advertising or product endorsement purposes.

The author and Steve Parish Publishing do not warrant or assume any legal liability or responsibility for the accuracy, completeness, or usefulness of any information, apparatus, product, or process disclosed.

Photographic Details

I began my career using only medium format cameras, 6x6 Yashica, Rolliflex and Hasselblad. I then changed to Nikon 35 mm SLR and then 35 mm for flowers and animals. I use 6x7 and 6x17 for landscapes. Now, with the major development of digital cameras and the software for post-production, I exclusively use DSLR cameras. I share this merely as a point of interest because camera brands, models of cameras and so on don't make my pictures — I do! For you, these choices are entirely personal, and dependent on opportunity, budget and your requirements for the end use.

Acknowledgements

Wildlife photography is often a team activity, and I would like to give a special acknowledgement to: Ian Morris, Dr Les Hall, the staff and management of the Narrowleaf Wildlife Shelter, the staff at Healesville Sanctuary, the staff and management of the Australian Wildlife Conservancy, New South Wales National Parks & Wildlife Service, Management of the Northern Territory Top End and Red Centre Wildlife Parks, and also to John and Caroline Hamilton of the Tasmanian Devil Conservation Park.

Published by Steve Parish Publishing Pty Ltd
PO Box 1058, Archerfield, Qld 4108 Australia
www.steveparish.com.au

ISBN 9781741933307

First published 2008

Principal photographer: Steve Parish

Additional photography: John Cann: p. 98; Greg Harm, SPP: p. 20 (left); Ian Morris: p. 77 (top left and centre left)

Photographs of equipment generously supplied by Maxwell Optical Industries Pty Ltd (Lowepro™ Bags, Velbon Tripods, Nikon)

Adobe product screen shots reprinted with permission from Adobe Systems Incorporated.

Front cover image: Bridled Nailtail Wallaby, Greg Harm, SPP

Title page main image: Sugar Glider on Banksia flower. Inset, top to bottom: Silhouette of a Green Tree-frog; Blue Tiger Butterfly

Text: Steve Parish
Design: Gill Stack, SPP
Editing: Kerry McDuling & Ted Lewis; Michele Perry, Karin Cox, Helen Anderson, SPP
Production: Tina Brewster, SPP

Prepress by Colour Chiefs Digital Imaging, Brisbane, Australia
Printed in Singapore by Imago

Produced in Australia at the Steve Parish Publishing Studios